Bea Season

B. D. JOHNSON

Dedicated to my grandchildren —
Noelle, Wyatt, Logan,
Lucy, Eleanore, Miles and Clara

CHAPTER 1

It was a pleasant afternoon in late spring. Small white butterflies darted among the ruffled marigolds edging the walk leading to the house. A black and white cat appeared briefly at the side yard fence, padding along the top rail in the awkward, swinging gait peculiar to a mother cat that has recently given birth.

On the front porch of the house, twelve-year-old Bea Lamb, christened Beatrice Isabel Lamb, sat in the swing hanging from chains secured to the porch rafters. The hem of her cotton print dress covered her knees. A faint line near the hem showed where the dress had been let down. From her place on the swing, the toes of her scuffed brown shoes didn't quite reach the ground.

A short while earlier, Bea had arched her foot and pushed lightly against the plank floor, setting the swing into gentle motion. She'd pulled her chin-length black hair away from her face and tucked it behind her ears. Then, settling back, her body relaxed and softened and her hands grew still at her sides. A small sigh passed her lips just before she'd closed her eyes in sleep.

Now, directly behind her, the kitchen window rattled briefly before the lower sash lifted in a series of jerks and screeches.

Bea's eyelids fluttered. But she wasn't truly awakened until three dark lumps sailed out through the open window and past her face, leaving a trace of warmed air along her cheek.

Still groggy and damp with sleep, Bea scooted off the porch swing, tilting the seat and spilling newspaper sheets onto the floor. Only a lucky grab prevented her from dropping the bowl of garden peas lying forgotten on her lap.

A sharp, burnt odor drifted across the porch. Bea sniffed curiously several times, then wrinkled her nose. A thin wisp of black smoke rose from the ground just beyond the porch.

With the bowl propped against her hip, Bea stepped across the scattered newspapers to the porch railing. Following the trail of smoke, she spotted two black lumps partially buried in the wet earth. A third lump had split open, spilling it's brown, steaming contents across the grass.

At first glance Bea was puzzled, but quickly her expression changed to one of startled recognition. Potatoes! The smoking lumps were tonight's supper. After arriving home from school, she'd put the potatoes in the oven to roast before moving outside to the porch swing to shell peas.

Staring at the ruined potatoes in dismay, Bea wiped her damp palm on the skirt of her dress. She hadn't meant to forget them. She hadn't planned on falling asleep. How could this happen so soon after promising her father she'd do better? If only she hadn't spotted today's newspaper rolled up and lying on the porch steps.

A children's story, published as a serial in the daily newspaper, had been the one bright spot in Bea's life during the past winter, and now into spring. While reading, she could temporarily forget the burdens that pressed so heavily on her heart. She anxiously awaited the arrival of each new installment.

The story was titled, *Perils in Paris*. The heroine, Juliette, lived in Paris, France, in the year 1900. She resided on a street of brick row houses, in the fourth floor loft of number nine. From this small peaked room Juliette looked out over the rooftops of the city and more directly onto a stone water fountain in the plaza below. But the most astonishing thing was that Juliette was a private detective.

Bea often daydreamed about living in Paris. She'd share Juliette's loft, join in her perilous escapades, and prove to be her trusted partner in solving crime. It was one of these daydreams that had led her to fall asleep instead of shelling peas.

Bea was still standing at the porch railing when she heard the front door open. She turned around slowly, knowing she'd run out of excuses.

Edward Lamb, Beatrice's father, stood in the open doorway. He was tall and lean with a thin honest face. His light brown hair was wavy and mussed; stubborn hair that defied his efforts to slick it back before he left the house each morning. His upper lip, even when he spoke, remained hidden behind a thick brown mustache.

Bea tilted her head to look into his face, expecting to hear angry, harsh words. Instead, they only sounded tired and disappointed.

"You're supposed to be tending to dinner. Not sitting out here daydreaming. You've ruined the last of the potatoes. Unless you think you can dream up a few."

"I'm sorry, Daddy. I only meant to sit here and shell the peas."

"Sorry doesn't put food on the table."

Bea hugged the bowl to her chest and ducked back inside the house. She knew her father already regretted the confrontation when he squeezed her shoulder gently as she passed through the door.

Edward dropped his hand and moved outside to sit on the porch steps, letting the screen slam shut.

On the sidewalk in front of the house, neighborhood children chased back and forth. Their high pitched calls and laughter befitting the last day of the school year and the beginning of summer vacation.

Edward barely noticed. His fingers combed absently through his hair; his gaze fixed on a spot between his feet.

He was weary and preoccupied with the weight and pull of difficult decisions. He questioned himself. Was he too hard on Bea, expecting too much? Wasn't it a father's responsibility to teach his children how to handle both the good times and bad? He felt the sting of his own disappointments; both in himself and in the news he had to break to his children tonight at dinner.

The kitchen was warm and stuffy with lingering smoke. Bea sat on a chair with the bowl of peas squeezed between her knees. Lifting one pod at a time she used her index finger to split open the skin and scrap out the peas she tossed into a cooking pot.

The peas were leftovers from her father's grocery store. Peas no one else had bought. Bea picked through the pile, eyeing them carefully to avoid the ones with brown spots or moldy skin.

Bea knew her father was right when he accused her of daydreaming. But, it was only in her daydreams that her world felt comfortable.

That's where her mother, Isabel, was at home cooking

the family's dinner. And every Sunday you could count on a chocolate cake waiting in the pantry for dessert. That's where her father's shirts were starched and pressed, and he didn't have to roll the sleeves to hide the frayed cuffs.

That's where she had time to play with her friends after school, instead of coming home to do chores. That's where her dad smiled a lot, and her mom sewed in the evenings while the family listened to the Biltmore Orchestra on the radio.

Outside her daydreams, Bea's mother remained a patient at the tuberculosis hospital in Salem, fifty miles south of the Lamb's home in Portland, Oregon. Children weren't allowed to visit, so neither Bea or her older brother Billy, had seen their mother in more than a year.

On Sunday afternoons, as often as he could afford the gasoline, Edward drove the one hundred mile round trip to the hospital to visit his wife. As Isabel's health improved, she wrote letters home. The first thing Bea did after arriving home from school each day was lift the lid of the tin box nailed to the front door and reach inside. She knew if she pulled out an envelope baring her mother's flowery handwriting, she'd find three pages inside: one for Edward, one for Billy and one for Bea. Bea saved all of hers.

After tossing the last few peas into the pot, Bea added a splash of water from the tap and set the pot on the stove to simmer. She retrieved three left over pork chops from the refrigerator and sprinkled them with generous amounts of salt. These she placed in a skillet to warm up.

A grease-spattered calendar hung on the wall in back of the stove. Remembering it was the first day of a new month Bea lifted it off the wall and flipped the page.

Across the top of the clean page, JUNE, 1935, was printed in bold, black letters. Below the date was a photograph: A wooden basket filled to overflowing with plump, red strawberries. Bea didn't need to look to know what was written at the bottom of the page:

Courtesy of Lamb's Grocery, Portland, Oregon.

She rehung the calendar over the bent nail.

Turning back to the stove, Bea considered the dinner of meat and peas. Without potatoes, Bea was worried Billy would complain. Hoping to fill him up, and at the same time prevent him from reminding her father about the lack of potatoes, she stacked sliced bread on a plate and set it on the table alongside a jar of jam, a bowl of sliced cucumbers, and a pitcher of milk. Finally she slid the pork chops onto a plate and drained the peas into a serving bowl.

With the table set, Bea stepped to the window and looked out onto the porch. Her fifteen-year-old brother, Billy, had come home and was sitting on the steps talking with their father.

From her vantage point, Bea looked at the back of their heads. Her father's unruly, light brown curls were mirrored on the head of his son.

Bea rapped on the window.

Billy turned at the sound and immediately jumped up. He had his father's hair all right, but his eyes were dark brown like his mother's. It was Bea who had her father's blue eyes.

Billy entered the kitchen with the cheerful swagger that went hand in hand with his love of food.

"I hope dinner is good, I'm starved."

He bypassed the table to wash his hands at the kitchen sink and was still drying them on a towel made from flour sacking when he slid into his chair.

Billy and Bea sat across from each other at the square kitchen table, their father on the side in-between. The remaining chair at the table was empty. A silent, empty place, that spoke loudly to the three seated at the table.

Edward took a moment to loosen the knot in his narrow black tie before he grasped each of his children by the hand and bowed to pray.

During the supper prayer, Bea kept her free hand in her lap, absently twisting her fingers in the fabric of her dress. She wondered what Billy did with his free hand.

A split second after the "Amen" Billy was smothering a piece of bread with strawberry jam. Bea picked up her fork and started on her peas.

"Hey, Dad," Billy said, "You don't mind if I go over to Henry's house after dinner? His parents are going out, so we can practice our music over there without bothering anyone. Gosh, Dad, wait until you hear our new numbers. I do a solo part that almost sounds like Benny Goodman, if I do say so myself."

"Don't talk so fast. You forget to chew," Edward remarked.

Bea picked up her knife and started on her chop.

"Billy, can I come and hear you practice?" she asked.

Billy held up his finger, postponing his reply until he'd drained his glass of milk in a succession of loud, breathy gulps. He set his glass back onto the table and let out a satisfied sigh.

"Sorry, no girls. It's just us guys." he said.

Their talk flowed around their father, who sat hunched over his plate, methodically taking bites.

"Guess what, Billy," said Bea. "When I was walking home from school today, Mrs. Payton was in her front yard. She says her cat had kittens yesterday. They're in a box in the shed. She said we could come over any time and look."

"I'm too busy tonight. Will ya pass the jam?"

Bea frowned, but held out the jar. Food was her toughest

competitor for Billy's attention.

"You might try saving some for the rest of us," Bea scolded. "Any way, I sure wish I could have one of those kittens."

Bea kept up her one sided conversation with Billy while secreting glances at her father. The expression on his face remained slack and distant. Bea saw little that resembled the jovial storyteller of the past. A past before mother got sick, before the hospital and the empty chair.

Bea hoped he wasn't missing the potatoes.

Billy finished off his third slice of bread and jam and reached for the milk pitcher to refill his glass.

"Did you hear about the kittens, Daddy?" Bea asked, looking directly at her father.

"I heard."

"Would you like a kitten?"

Before he could answer, Billy interrupted.

"Thanks for supper," he pushed his chair back from the

"I gotta get my clarinet and run."

Bea glared across the table at Billy.

"It's your turn to wash."

"Dishes are girl's work. I've got important things to do tonight. Do you think Benny Goodman got famous by staying home and washing dishes?"

"Daddy, tell Billy he has to help."

Before answering, Edward tipped his chair back and stretched out his legs. He rubbed his upper lip with the forefinger on his left hand, brushing the bristly edge of his mustache; a habit that allowed him space to gather his thoughts.

"Sit still Billy," he finally said. In a resigned manner he dropped his hands to his thighs.

Billy turned his chair around before returning to his seat. He crossed his arms over the back of the chair and rested his chin there.

8

"Dad, couldn't I skip the dishes this once?"

"This isn't about dishes, Billy. I have something of great importance to discuss with both of you."

CHAPTER 2

Edward leaned into the table and clasped his hands. Then for the first time since the family sat down to supper, he looked into the faces of his children. His eyebrows lifted and he smiled, giving out a hopeful, yet guarded, look.

Throughout dinner Bea had been sneaking glances at her father, anxious to discover the reason he remained so aloof and preoccupied. To see his familiar smile brought immediate relief.

"Daddy, today is the first of June," Bea said. "The doctor said Mommy might be able to come home in June. Is that what you wanted to tell us?"

"Well, I did talk to the doctor. He assured me that your mother's on the mend. Her lungs are almost clear of tuberculosis. A result of the good Lord's fortune I'll not deny."

"I just knew she'd get well," Bea leaped from her chair and rushed around the table, aiming to hug Billy.

"Ah, Bea," Billy whined, while playfully swatting her away.

Bea managed to poke him in the side before scooting behind her father and wrapping her arms around his neck.

"Maybe we'll finally get some decent food," Billy joked,

scrunching up the dishtowel he'd used for a napkin and pelting Bea with it.

"Mom's finally coming home," Bea sang, "Mom's finally coming home." The sound of the words lifted her spirits.

While Bea draped the dishtowel, shawl-like, across her shoulders, Billy was watching his father with a growing awareness that this conversation was about something more than their mother's homecoming.

Holding the shawl out like wings, Bea set off across the kitchen floor in a series of twirling pirouettes. Coming to a shaky stop beside her father, she asked, "Daddy, is mom coming home this weekend? Do Billy and I get to go with you to pick her up?"

"Cut out the questions and let him finish," Billy said. "What's the matter Dad? Isn't Mom coming home? You said she was as good as well."

"She is, Billy." Edward paused, his back stiffened as he took a deep breath. "Just to be safe, the doctor feels she should stay in the hospital through the summer."

"Not come home this summer?" For a few seconds Bea squeezed her eyes shut, as if by doing so she could shield herself from the shock of her father's words. Her hand slipped from his shoulder. She stepped back, sinking into her chair.

"But, Daddy, that's not fair," she said. Mom can't miss summer; and, and… I was planning on her." Bea's face crumpled with disappointment, her eyes prickled and pooled with water. She blinked rapidly to keep the tears from overflowing.

"I know it's a terrible disappointment," Edward said.

"Remember now, we all knew there was only a possibility she'd be able to come home this soon. Missing Mom as much as we did it was easy to hope for too much.

"What's important now is that we all pull together for

just a few more weeks. The summer will be over before we know it. Meanwhile, there are going to be a few temporary changes. You see, I've decided to close the store."

"But you close the store every night," Bea said.

"This time I won't be opening in the morning. I've decided to close the store for the entire summer. If things work out, well, I might be able to open again in September.

"You both know that people across the country are struggling to make ends meet during this depression. Things will change, get better. But for now, I can't make enough profit at the store to pay bills.

With cash money hard to come by, the people who can will grow vegetable gardens so they won't need to buy from the grocer."

For a moment no one spoke. Edward feeling somewhat relieved now that he'd delivered the unwelcome news to his children. He eased back in his seat, slowly circling his shoulders to ease his taut muscles. Though he feared that what he had to say next might be even more difficult for Billy and Bea to accept.

"Dad," if you don't open the store, where will you work? "What are you going to do?" Billy asked.

"I've had an offer of a job at a garage in Springfield, Oregon. The job's mine if I show up there Monday morning. You kids know Mike, the butcher. His brother owns the garage. He says the drought and dust storms in the midwest are forcing a lot of people to leave their homes, pack up their belongings and head to the west coast looking for summer work; most of them driving broken down cars. With the increase in repair business he's looking to take on extra help for the summer.

"You mean we're all moving to Springfield?" Billy asked.

Bea's voice quivered, "Daddy, we can't move even farther away from Mom." Bea wanted to cover her ears, block out

13

her father's answer. Could things get any worse?

"Springfield's not much farther from Salem than we are here, just lies in a different direction. What I need to explain to you children is that I'm the only one going to Springfield. The two of you are staying here."

Edward raised his hands, as if to hold off the protests he expected would follow this latest bit of news.

"You see, I've known for several months that I might have to close the store. Isabel and I have discussed this. If I go to Springfield alone, I can fix a small living area in the back of the garage and save almost all my wages.

"You know I can't leave the two of you here alone."

"Is someone coming to stay with us?" Billy asked.

"Well, nooo. You've both heard your mother talk about her childhood friend, Lila Bishop. It seems Lila recently moved back to Oregon. She works east of town, at the county poor farm. Lila's agreed to let you stay with her for the summer."

Billy and Bea exchanged horrified looks.

"The Poor Farm?" Billy spat out, his voice cracked with emotion. "You can't send us to live at the poor farm. What if my friends find out? Dad, people make jokes about that place. People who end up there are said to be lazy and no-good."

"Billy it's not like that. Lila just happens to work there. She lives with the superintendent and his family in a very nice house on the grounds."

"Why can't I come with you?" Billy pleaded. "I'm fifteen. I'm old enough to work with you at the garage."

"The offer was for work for one man. And besides, like I already said, if I go alone I can save almost all my wages.

"Billy, you need to stay and finish the last week of high school. Bea's school let out today, but don't think I've forgotten you have final exams next week. I've already talked to Mrs. Payton. She's agreed to let you stay with them until school closes and then you can join your sister.

"You both might find you like living out in the country. Lila said there'd be work for both of you."

Bea watched Billy. She needed him to sit up and smile like everything was fine, say something funny. Anything to make her believe she hadn't heard right, this bad thing wasn't really happening. But Billy only stared sullenly at the table, flicking his finger at a pea lodged under the edge of his plate.

"How are you getting to Springfield?" Billy asked.

"Hitch a ride, I hope. There's folks willing to give me a lift if I offer to pay for gas. Or I can take the train."

"Now, the two of you better start packing while your "Old Pop" cleans up the dishes."

Billy got up. He knew there was no use in arguing. Besides, he was anxious to get out of sight before his dad changed his mind about the dishes.

Bea and Edward remained, listening to the sound of Billy's footsteps until they faded into silence behind his closed bedroom door.

When Bea stood and pushed in her chair, her father reached out, pulling her onto his lap.

"What's my favorite girl thinking?" he asked.

His soothing voice and gentle inquiry broke through Bea's fragile wall of denial. In a fluid motion of despair, she leaned into his chest, wrapped her arms around his neck, and began to sob.

Edward patiently waited, all the while his hand rubbed circles on her back and he murmured, "there now."

When her flow of tears was exhausted Bea loosened her hold around her father's neck and sat up. Edward pulled a handkerchief from his inside jacket pocket and handed it to

15

her. She wiped her eyes and blew her nose while Edward smoothed her hair back from her face. Bea responded with a trembling smile.

"That's my girl," Edward said. "You've been such a trooper. Did you know your mother insists that knowing you were here taking such good care of Billy and me helped her get well?"

"Really, Daddy?"

"Scout's honor. I know it hasn't been easy being the only woman in the house. And I know you've been making plans for this summer when mom came home. It really hurts to accept that's not going to happen."

Bea nodded and blew her nose.

"Instead of dwelling on your disappointment, try looking upon this summer as a well-earned vacation.

"Lila took care of your mom when your mom was a girl. When I talked to Lila on the telephone, Lila told me she considers it a great favor for us to let you kids come for the summer. She never married and always thought of your mom as her adopted daughter."

"I guess that would make us her adopted grandchildren."

"I guess that's exactly what she's thinking," Edward said.

"I know it'd mean a lot to your mother if you kids became good friends with Lila. Now, you had better hop up and start packing."

Edward set Bea on her feet. Her chest rose and fell with the shaky breaths that follow a good cry. Edward began clearing the table. He carried a stack of dishes to the sink and turned the hot water on over the dishpan.

"I'll take you out to Lila's in the morning."

"Okay Daddy."

Bea knew the minister at church taught that it was every-one's duty, no matter what happens, to find something good.

16

Bea didn't think she was very good at duty. Hadn't she tried for more than a year to find something good about her mother's tuberculosis? Now she wouldn't have a mother, a father, or a home. Not even a minister should expect duty to cover all that.

As she turned to leave the kitchen, her father called out.

"Wait, I almost forgot to give you this." With his wet, soapy fingers he carefully worked an envelope out of his back pants pocket. He used his pant leg to wipe away the soap bubbles he'd dripped on the envelope.

"Your mom asked me to give you this. She thought it'd help."

Back in her bedroom, Bea sat on her bed, holding the envelope on her lap. The letters of her name were smeared where the soap had blurred the ink. Bea's chest tightened at the sight of her mother's familiar handwriting.

CHAPTER 3

Early the next morning, father and daughter set off down the sidewalk, walking the five blocks to the street corner where they would board the electric trolley. Bea carried a paper box tied with string. Her father carried her cardboard suitcase.

As they approached their destination, Bea heard the clang, clang, of a trolley bell. In this part of the city, trolley car tracks ran down the center of the street. Automobiles passed on both sides, going in opposite directions.

Hugging her box to her chest, Bea ran ahead of her father. She was anxious to arrive at the crosswalk where she could see into the street.

She found a spot at the curb next to a tall woman accompanied by two poodles on leash.

The woman wore a red, nubby wool coat and shiny red shoes with narrow heels. On her head set a round, red hat with a black feather poking up in the front and red netting that swept across her forehead. She glanced at Bea and smiled, her upturned lips prominent under a slick covering of glossy, red lipstick.

When Bea had arrived at the curb, the two white poodles were lying quietly at the woman's feet with their chins resting on their front paws, and the tips of their pink tongues protruding between their lips. Now they were on their feet yapping and pulling on their leashes. Their small bodies quivering for attention while sniffing and licking Bea's shoes.

"Well, hello there." Bea bent down to pat the furry puffs on the tops of their heads.

When Bea looked back to the street, a trolley car was there, stopped on the tracks. As she watched, doors at both ends of the car folded back. People milling next to the tracks separated into two lines and shuffled toward the open doors.

Bea turned and looked for her father.

"Hurry, Daddy, we'll miss the trolley."

"No need to worry, Bea. That trolley is headed downtown. The one we want will be going in the other direction. So, you might as well pull up a chair while we wait," Edward said, gesturing toward the suitcase he'd set on the pavement.

Bea wondered if the lady might let her hold one of the poodles on her lap. As she moved to sit down there came the sharp, slapping sound of footsteps moving up the sidewalk in their direction. Without ever slowing, a man sprinted past, hurdling the dogs without breaking stride.

Bea was so startled she slipped off the end of the suitcase and landed hard on the rough edge of the cement curb. The man was now into the street, zigzagging between cars at the traffic stop, all the while waving one hand in the air and using his other to secure his hat.

The trolley had just begun to move when he reached it. He leaped, landing one foot on the bottom step and grabbing the handrail beside the door. He slipped inside the car just ahead of the closing door. Only the tail end of his coat was caught and left hanging outside.

Bea scrambled to her feet, rubbing her backside.

"Well…Well…" Edward sputtered.

"I never." the lady remarked.

The sharp, staccato yipping of the two, startled poodles added to the commotion.

The lady in red was becoming hopelessly entangled as the two dogs ran in frenzied circles around her legs. She struggled to maintain her balance without losing hold of the leashes.

"Did that big, bad man scare my little darlings?" she cooed, leaning down and trying to calm the dogs.

The way the feather on her hat dipped and bobbed along with the motion of her head reminded Bea of a big, red bird pecking at a worm.

Watching, Bea laughed aloud, while Edward tried to suppress a smile and they both reached in to help untangle the dogs.

Out in the street, another trolley arrived.

"Looks like our ride's here," Edward said.

After giving the two furry heads a final pat, Bea tugged on her father's hand, "Hurry, Daddy."

Bea was first in line to board the trolley. The moment the door opened she stepped inside, squeezing between the passengers getting off. She chose an empty seat in the center of the car and scooted in close to the window.

Today's trip was only the second occasion for Bea to ride on a trolley. The first had been a family outing to downtown Portland to look at the Christmas displays in the department store windows. Most places she needed to go, she walked. Although on Sundays, the family sometimes rode to church in the delivery truck.

Edward came aboard at a more leisurely pace and sat next to Bea. Bea perched on the edge of her seat, twisting around to watch the other passengers board.

The tightly woven wicker seat made the backs of Bea's knees feel scratchy. So she took off her sweater and spread it over the seat to act as a cushion.

The doors at both ends of the car closed, the bell rang, and the trolley began to roll.

Bea had grown up playing in neighborhoods where trolleys routinely passed. Today, Bea realized that riding inside the trolley, looking out at all the familiar streets and buildings, created a pleasantly odd sensation; Like suddenly finding yourself inside the bathroom mirror, looking out.

Bea settled back into her seat, relishing this moment of shared adventure with her father. When she slipped her hand around his coat sleeve, he reached across his lap and rested his hand on her arm.

Until that moment, Bea had been caught up in the novelty of the trolley ride and had managed to push aside thoughts regarding the real reason for the day's journey. But now, the weight and warmth of her father's presence beside her triggered the return of all the pent up fears from the night before. A lump rose in her throat, her stomach twisted into a tight, hard knot.

What would life on a poor farm be like?

What if Lila didn't like her?

What if she didn't like Lila?

From this end of things, an entire summer seemed like a very, very, long time. Bea bit her lower lip and stared out the window.

The further east the trolley rolled, the less familiar the scenery rushing past outside the window. Bea had always lived in the city, where buildings snuggled close and the neighborhood kids gathered in streets and empty lots for their games. Out here, it was the land that filled up the space.

Bea liked the way houses were scattered and settled at the

end of dirt lanes. Thick hedges of brush and wild berry vines wound fence-like between fields.

Edward and Bea rode in companionable silence. Both content to watch the changing countryside.

They had traveled several miles when an unusual sight caught Bea's eye. She leaned toward the window and pressed her face to the glass.

"Daddy, what is that?"

Edward leaned toward the window.

Bordering the track on both sides, were fields that appeared to be sprouting poles: hundreds, even thousands, of tall wood poles, rising fifteen feet into the sky. The poles were sorted into rows, evenly spaced and connected by thick wires strung across their tops. Between poles, strings stretched up from the ground and were tied to the high wire.

Edward looked over Bea's shoulder. He nodded and rubbed his upper lip.

"The first time I saw a field like that, I was about your age. When I asked what they were for my papa said, 'those poles mark the spot where a Giant plants his garden. Giant green beans and peas grow up those strings.'"

Edward's voice maintained a serious tone, but Bea didn't miss the teasing sparkle in his eyes.

"No, really Daddy."

"You don't need to worry," Edward added, "only the friendliest kind of giants bother with a garden."

Bea pursed her lips and set both hands on her hips, staring up at her father with a look that clearly conveyed she was much too old to believe that.

Edward chuckled and ruffled Bea's hair.

"Bea, that is a hop field. Those green clumps on the ground at the base of the strings are hop vines. In a few more weeks, those vines will have climbed to the top of the strings and spilled over the wire. By August, they'll be covered in pale, green blossoms. Then the vines will be cut down. A work crew will pick off the blossoms and store them in large wicker baskets."

"Did you ever pick the blossoms, Daddy?"

"A few times. It's mighty hard work for a small wage. Why, those blossoms are as light as feathers and the pickers are paid by the weight of the blossoms in their basket."

"What do they do with the blossoms?"

"They use them to make beer."

"I thought maybe they crushed them to make perfume."

Edward shook his head, "I'm afraid it wouldn't be a very pleasant smelling perfume."

"Why? What do they smell like?"

"Well, like nothing else really, just like hops."

When the mysterious hop field was out of sight, Bea settled back in her seat. Hop fields gave way to plowed fields and grazing cattle.

Occasionally a road crossed the tracks. Each time this happened, the conductor slowed the trolley and rang the warning bell as they approached.

Alongside the track at one of these crossings was a pasture, fenced in with barbed wire. In the pasture a freckle faced boy wearing overalls, stood on the bare back of a shaggy, brown horse. He waved both arms above his head at the passing trolley. Bea returned his wave. The horse kept his nose buried in a bucket on the ground and never looked up.

Forty minutes after leaving the familiar corner near Bea's house the trolley arrived at the end of the track. From here, the trolley headed back to the city.

Edward dragged the suitcase from underneath the seat and stepped into the aisle.

"We're here. This is our stop Bea."

24

Bea stood and slipped on her sweater before retrieving her box. She pictured the things she'd carefully packed inside: All of her mother's letters, including the letter her father had given her last night, stationery and stamps, and at the top of the pile a family photograph, taken three years ago at a fourth of July picnic.

In the black and white photograph, Bea and her parents were seated on a blanket in a grassy field, each holding a thick slice of watermelon. Bea is leaning over her plate, mouth open, ready to take a bite. Edward is looking directly at the camera. Isabel has one hand lifted to the side of her face, brushing her hair out of the way while she eats.

A partial view of Billy appears in the upper right hand corner of the photograph. He's biting into a slice of watermelon while hanging upside down. Neither the tree nor the branch he is draped over are visible in the photograph, which gives the appearance he is magically suspended in the air. A feat Billy is quite proud to claim.

Reluctantly Bea follows her father down the aisle, with the knowledge that she would soon be left in the care of a total stranger settling over her like a blanket of gloom, weighting her steps.

At the end of the line only three passengers remained aboard the trolley: Bea, Edward, and an old man in a tattered flannel coat. The man had a long, frizzy grey beard that he tucked inside his coat between the top two buttons. He stepped off the trolley and walked away in a shuffling, yet determined gait. He kept his head down, chin pressed to his chest as if the weight of his beard held it there.

A short distance beyond the track Edward and Bea crossed a two-lane highway.

"Up there, that's where we're headed," Edward said.

Bea looked in the direction he was pointing. In the

distance she could see the white domed top of a water tower, the pitched roof of a large barn and patches of color that hinted at other buildings hidden among the trees.

Beyond the highway, the passing of many feet had pressed a path through a field of the knee-high grass. The path appeared to lead to the distant buildings. The only person in sight along the path was the old man from the trolley.

"Look's like we three have the same destination," Edward said. He shifted the suitcase to his other hand and set out after the old man.

A car driving down the road from the east, slowed and pulled to a stop beside Bea. The passenger in the front seat climbed out. He waved goodbye to the driver and boarded the trolley.

As Bea watched, the conductor rose from his seat and walked the length of the trolley to an identical seat at the other end. In the funny, topsy-turvy way of trolleys, the back had now become the front for the return trip to the city.

Bea turned and hurried after her father.

The path led through grassy fields until it eventually opened into a clearing of packed dirt in front of a towering three-story, brick building. White painted porches littered with rocking chairs and small tables, were stacked one above the other and spanned nearly half of that side of the building. Wide wooden steps led up to the lower porch and a pair of doors.

Edward turned away from the brick building and approached a house situated a short distance to the west. The house was white with dark green shutters. A garage on the south side of the house opened into the clearing. A white picket fence enclosed the house and its neatly clipped front yard.

Edward passed through a gate in the fence and followed a path of flat stones sunk into the grass leading to the front porch. Arriving at the front door, Edward set down the suitcase and pulled a handkerchief from his back pants pocket. He wiped his face while he stretched and circled his shoulders to ease the strain.

Bea's steps slowed and came to a stop just outside the gate. She hugged her box. She couldn't ignore the eerie feeling that once she stepped through the gate she was leaving behind forever, a familiar part of herself.

"Come on Bea, don't stand there all day," Edward called back to her. "I'm ready to ring the bell."

"I'm coming." She tried to shake off a shiver of dread.

Passing through the gate and under the arched trellis, Bea hurried up the stone path. Edward knocked on the door. With her shoulder pressed close to her father's side, Bea waited for the door to open.

CHAPTER
4

Waiting outside the front door, Bea tensed and straightened her shoulders at the faint clicking sound of approaching heeltaps from inside the house. Edward cleared his throat.

A woman opened the door. She wore a sheer, blue print dress that, except for the collar and sleeves, was hidden beneath a starched white apron tied about her waist. Her eyes were light gray and she wore her thick white hair rolled and crimped and nestled on her head like a crown. Her face was round and her cheeks rosy. She greeted them with the broad, easy smile of a person who is perpetually good-natured.

"Edward, Beatrice, come in."

Bea couldn't move. She felt like she was floating above legs and feet too heavy to lift. Edward picked up the suitcase and started Bea forward with a gentle push on the small of her back.

After their time spent outdoors, the light in the house seemed dim and the air felt cool.

"Edward, I'm so glad to finally meet you in person. And welcome to you too Beatrice," the woman said. "You've probably figured out I'm, Lila. I can't tell you how glad I am to have you staying with me this summer."

Bea replied, "Thank you," but wondered if she was expected to say that she was glad too. Instead she added, "You can call me Bea."

"Bea it is."

While Lila and Bea talked, Edward nervously fingered his hat, sliding it through his fingers like a slowly revolving wheel.

"Edward, can I get you a cup of coffee? I've a fresh pot in the kitchen."

"I thank you Lila," he said, in response to her offer, "but no, I've got a bit of hitching and hiking to do if I'm going to be in Springfield, Monday morning. I'd better get started."

Edward shuffled his feet and rubbed his upper lip.

Bea looked down at her hand where she was slowly wrapping one finger in a tail of string hanging from the knot on top of her box.

Lila waited, her arms crossed in a hug around her ample chest.

All three waiting, postponing the word or step that would take Edward away.

Finally, Edward let out a deep sigh. He squared his shoulders and slapped the side of his leg with his hat.

"Can't tell you how much I appreciate you helping us out Lila," he said, while extending his hand.

She gave his hand a firm shake. "My pleasure."

Bea squeezed both arms around her father's waist and buried her face in his shirtfront. She didn't want to let go of his solid warmth. After he kissed the top of her head, she reluctantly dropped her arms and stepped back.

Lila was holding the front door open. Edward turned and walked outside.

When he reached the gate he turned and looked back at the house. "I'll send you my address as soon as I get settled, Bea."

"Okay Daddy, bye."

Bea sucked on her trembling lower lip, fighting the desire to rush out the door and beg her father to take her with him.

"Bye, Sweetie. Remember, Billy will be here Saturday."

Bea stood next to Lila in the doorway and watched her father walk away. When he reached the far side of the clearing, he put on his hat and without turning, lifted his arm over his head to wave goodbye.

Bea followed Lila back inside the house.

Lila nodded toward the staircase that dominated the front hall, "The first thing we need to do is take your things up to your bedroom. I don't know if your father told you, but there are three families sharing this house. We all use the same front door, but the house is divided so we have our own apartments.

"Mr. and Mrs. Briggs, the administrator and his wife, live on the first floor. The door to their apartment is there, behind you. Remember, you can't just barge into their rooms; you must knock first.

I hope you will become good friends with their son, Walter. In fact," Lila raised her voice, "he's probably trying to watch us through the keyhole right now."

Having said this, Lila picked up Bea's suitcase and started upstairs.

Bea glanced over her shoulder at the Briggs' door. She imagined a huge, blinking eye on the other side of the keyhole, like the eye in the Cyclops picture in her literature book. The image lightened her mood and allowed a small smile to appear on her face.

Along with the smile, Bea felt some of her loneliness fade; replaced with a new-found curiosity about Walter.

31

In imitation of her father, she let out a deep sigh, slapped the side of her leg, and hurried up the stairs after Lila.

The top of the staircase opened onto a large, square landing. The wood floor was bare and polished to a high gleam. Sunlight entered through a window directly across from the staircase, giving the area a warm and welcoming feel.

Framed photographs bordered the window. Later on, when Bea had a chance to study the photographs, she discovered they were all taken during the construction of the county poor farm in 1911.

The door to the right of the stairs was narrowly open, revealing a sliver of light from the room beyond. When Bea looked in that direction, the door closed with a soft click. The door to Bea's left was closer to the stairs and wide open. Lila was inside and called out the door to Bea.

"Miss Virginia Grim has the apartment across the hall. She's head of the nursing staff for the residents here at the farm. I'm sure you'll meet her later. Be on your best behavior when you do."

Although Lila spoke about Miss Grim in the casual relaxed manner Bea would learn suited Lila's nature, Bea couldn't shake the feeling that Lila's final words held a trace of warning. A warning about what, she wondered. Bea looked back at Miss Grim's closed door; there was nothing there to provide her with a clue.

Lila spread her arms in a welcoming gesture. "Well, come on in," she said, "get acquainted with your new home."

Bea shook off her puzzling thoughts about Miss Grim, and nervously stepped inside the apartment that was to become her summer home.

"I call this, 'My sit and do everything' room," Lila said. "Behind that screen is the kitchen. Further back you'll find my bedroom, the bathroom, and the stairs to the attic. That's where you'll be sleeping. It's only an unfinished attic, but I fixed it up. When your brother arrives he'll be sleeping at the dormitory with the men.

Bea nodded to show she was listening, but didn't comment. Bea was glad for the cushion of Lila's easy chatter. It softened the impact of taking in the new surroundings. Lila didn't seem to mind that Bea wasn't holding up her end of the conversation.

"Unless you have questions, I need to be getting to work. I don't usually work on Saturdays, but we had some supplies arrive early this morning and I have some paperwork to do. On weekdays I start work at 8:00, but I waited to greet you this morning.

"I'll leave you alone now to look around the apartment. On my way out I'll stop downstairs and ask Walter to come up and knock on the door in an hour. That should give you enough time to get settled.

"I know Walter's bustin' his britches to give you a tour of the grounds. Be sure he brings you over to my office."

Lila left, closing the door, only to reopen it a few seconds later. "One more thing, Bea. Those attic stairs are steep and kind of tricky. Be careful going up and down the first few times."

"I should know," Lila chuckled. She lifted the front of her skirt to reveal her knees. The skin on both knees was bruised and mottled in varying shades of purple and yellow.

Bea automatically winced in surprise and sympathy.

"Stairs are for the young, not the young at heart," Lila quipped heartily, without any apparent resentment, and closed the door for the final time.

Left alone, Bea studied the contents of the apartment. Bea thought the furnishings unusual, but now she decided they had a very pleasing affect.

At the center of the room was a sofa with silky, fabric cushions in a startling shade of red. Its wood armrests and legs were decoratively carved and lacquered.

Bea crossed the room and gingerly sat on one of the cushions. It felt firm and slick. In front of the sofa was a trunk, draped with a white cloth edged in lace. Magazines were scattered on top.

Across from the sofa, there were two chairs: A well worn, brown leather rocker and a straight backed wood chair, painted yellow and made even brighter with lilac blooms stitched in needlepoint, covering the seat and footstool. Between the chairs there was a lamp on a round table.

In one corner of the room was a radio. Back home, Bea's family had a small radio they kept on top of a bookshelf. Lila's radio was almost as tall as a bedroom bureau, and stood by itself.

There was a built-in china hutch wedged into another corner. A large picture window on the west wall of the room was draped in sheer, lacy curtains that let in lots of light.

Bea scooted off the sofa, suddenly anxious to see the attic room where she'd sleep. First she peeked into the kitchen, hidden from view to the sitting area behind a bamboo screen. The screen was slightly higher than the top of Bea's head. Three silver bells tied into a braided rope hung across the top of the screen at one end. On the floor at the other end of the screen, stood a bamboo table and a plant with broad, pale green leaves, in a copper pot.

A table and two chairs sat next to the screen on the kitchen side.

An arched opening at the back of the kitchen led into a hall where Bea found her suitcase on the floor at the foot of a staircase. In the same hall were two doors. Through one of the doors Bea could see the corner of a bed. She guessed the other door led to the bathroom.

Bea set her box on top of the suitcase, deciding to return for both things later after she'd looked upstairs.

She'd seen attic stairs in her grandmother's house. But, they were usually out of sight, pushed up into the attic itself and lowered by pulling on a handle in the ceiling of the floor below. Bea noticed this staircase was intended to remain permanently lowered and had been nailed securely to the hall floor. The attached handrail was new, of a lighter wood than the steps and still carried the aroma of freshly cut wood.

Bea reached for the railing and started up. The steps were narrow and open at the back, the toes of her shoes poked over the edge. After climbing a few steps, she discovered that looking down at the receding floor, while climbing up, caused a floating, dizzy feeling. So, keeping a tight hold on the handrail, she continued the climb with her head tilted back. Which is why the first thing that caught her attention in the attic, was the ceiling.

Although quite high in the center of the room, it angled down sharply on all four sides, meeting side walls that were only waist high. At the ceilings highest point, hung a light fixture with a single, bare bulb. A string, tied to a thin chain on the fixture, passed through a series of cup hooks screwed into the ceiling and continued down the wall to within reach of the staircase. Bea tugged on the string and the light clicked on. She grinned and tugged it off.

The attic was a bright and cheerful space with a window in all three outside walls. To Bea's amusement, the unusually short walls placed the lower sill on each of the windows within inches of the floor. She would be able to sit on the floor and look directly out.

The room wore a fresh coat of white paint. The air still carried a faint odor of paint fumes and cleaning solution.

Though small the room held a desk and chair, a bed, a wood coat-stand with pegs, a bureau, and a lamp on a nightstand beside the bed. The only rug, a small braided oval, was placed to be underfoot when she climbed in or out of bed.

Bea wandered around the room, one hand drifting lightly over the furniture, then kneeling to look out the windows. Each window faced a different direction. A view of the dormitory to the east, barns and pastures to the south and to the west she could make out the highway that ran next to the trolley track.

Rising, she walked to the bed and sat down. The bedspread was yellow chenille, patterned with fuzzy threads. The mattress bowed gently under her weight and the bed springs emitted quiet, pinging sounds.

The freshly painted walls were bare except for a framed print at the head of the bed. Bea scooted over for a closer look.

The scene showed two young children, hands clasped, crossing the narrow footbridge spanning a swiftly, flowing stream. Above the children's heads, two angels in luminous gowns smiled and stretched out their arms, assuring safety.

Bea settled back into the center of the bed. She hugged her bent legs to her chest and rested her chin on her knees.

Why this isn't an attic at all, she thought. It's a loft. My own lovely loft, just like Juliette's loft in Paris.

Suddenly aware of how much time had passed, Bea slid off the bed and returned downstairs to retrieve her things. She hung her sweater on a peg and emptied the contents of the suitcase into the bureau drawers. The empty suitcase, she pushed under the bed.

She placed her box on the desk. The string she'd wrapped around the box and carefully tied in a bow, had been tugged and twisted into a tight knot. Bea spent several minutes of careful picking before the knot loosened and came undone.

The letters and the photograph remained just as she'd packed them the evening before. At the top of the stack was the most recent letter from her mother; the one she'd received only last night. She lifted the envelope from the pile and slipped out a single sheet of cream-colored paper, folded in half. Bea opened the letter and read.

My Dearest Bea,

I'm afraid I must write hurriedly, as your father's visit is almost over. I also hoped I would be going home today. I tell myself that the summer will pass quickly, yet it hurts to wait even a few more weeks.

In spite of the delay I am thankful. I am so fortunate to be healed. So many are not.

Just last night a new patient, a woman about my age, arrived. This morning, when I entered the sunroom, there she was sitting at an easel and painting a beautiful watercolor. She noticed me watching and offered to give me lessons.

I've always wanted to learn to paint but never believed I'd have the opportunity. I see this as God's way of softening the hurt He knew I'd feel when my plans to return home were delayed.

If you trust, even though what has happened seems unfair, I know you will find that God has something wonderful planned for you this summer.

Give my love to Lila. I will be looking forward to your letters.

Love, Mom

From downstairs came the sound of knocking.

Bea hastily slipped the letter back inside the envelope in the box. She opened a deep desk drawer, dropped in the box, and closed the drawer.

Her heart ached for her mother's presence, but her spirit was stirred by her mother's words about a God who had wonderful plans for even a girl like her.

Bea hurried downstairs to answer the door.

CHAPTER 5

Bea opened the apartment door to a boy wearing denim overalls. He kept his hands stuffed into his hip pockets while nervously shifting his weight from one foot to another. He had silky straight hair, bluntly cut, and so light blonde in color that you might imagine he was wearing a white bowl atop his head. In contrast to his pale hair, his face was tanned and freckled.

"Hello," Bea said, her inquisitive blue eyes looking directly into his mischievous brown ones.

"Hi. Are you ready?" he answered.

"Yeah, sure."

The boy, whom Bea could only assume was Walter, turned and started down the stairs.

Bea followed, after checking to be sure she had properly closed the door behind her. Following seems to be all I'm good for lately, she thought. I followed Daddy here. I followed Lila upstairs and now I'm following Walter back down.

She caught up with Walter when he stopped to grab two bowls sitting on top of a small table at the bottom of the stairs. He carried the two bowls outside and sat on the porch steps.

Bea, still following, sat down beside him. Walter handed her one of the bowls.

"It's gingerbread with whipped cream," he said. "We don't usually get to eat cake in the morning, but my mother made it especially for you."

The cake was still warm and Bea breathed in its spicy aroma. The dollop of whipped cream on top had begun to melt and run down the sides, where it pooled on the bottom of the bowl.

They both dug in their forks and began to eat.

"Did Lila say your name was Beet?" Walter finally asked after swallowing several large bites of cake.

"No, Bea, short for Beatrice."

"I like Beet. Maybe I'll call you Beet."

Walter looked over at Bea, his expression smug and challenging. He swiped one finger around the inside of his bowl to catch any last traces of cake.

Bea finished chewing and swallowed. Living with an older brother for twelve years had taught her how to maneuver out of a bad situation before it had the chance to get up a good head of steam.

"Did Lila say your name was Walter?"

"Yeah."

"I like Wart. Maybe I'll call you Wart."

Bea returned Walter's stare, while leisurely licking whipped cream off the back of her fork.

"You have whipped cream on your nose," she said.

Walter lifted his arm and angrily swiped at his nose with his sleeve.

"I didn't say I would, I said I might call you Beet."

"Oh."

Bea stood up, and this time it was Walter who followed.

"Well, give me your bowl," Walter said. Bea handed over

her empty bowl.

"Tell your mother it was very good."

Walter disappeared back inside the house and returned a moment later.

"Come on, I'll show you around."

They walked side by side down the porch steps, but when they came to the trellis over the gate, Bea let Walter go first. Bea had also learned that to remain on equal footing you had to know when to back down.

At the base of the trellis, Bea spotted a plant she hadn't noticed earlier. A small, green, leafy mound with tendrils climbing upward, winding through the wood slats.

"Walter, wait a minute. Do you know the name of this plant?"

"That's a hop vine. Why?"

"Just wondered."

Bea was secretly pleased. Now maybe she'd have the opportunity to pick some of the blossoms her father had told her about.

They continued walking in the direction of the large brick building.

"This is the dormitory," Walter explained. It's where all the people who come here to live eat and sleep."

Bea remembered that the dormitory was where Lila had said Billy would sleep.

"What are the people like?" she asked Walter. "A three story building must hold a lot of people." Bea was worried for Billy's sake.

"Just like people anywhere, I guess," Walter answered. Most of them are old, but friendly. Sometimes they seem sad. They miss the lives they had before the "hard times" changed everything. They miss their families."

Walter's answer made Bea uncomfortable. The "hard

41

times" he'd mentioned and other people referred to as "the depression" had forced her father to close his store. In her mind, "hard times" would always be connected with her mother's illness. Bea missed her family the way it used to be. She found herself fearful and defensive at the thought that the people living here at the county poor farm weren't really so different from herself.

Bea tipped her head back to view the dormitory's upper porches. Several men were sitting in the rocking chairs on the second floor. And on the third floor, Bea could see the dark hair on the bent head of a woman, rocking and gazing at something in her lap.

The dormitory had two front doors, both having etched, glass panels in the top half. With their hands framing their faces to block the glare, Walter and Bea leaned their foreheads against the glass and peered inside.

A wide, linoleum floored hall cut straight through the heart of the building to another set of doors at the far end. Numerous doors and narrow hallways branched off to the right and left. Just inside, on the left, was a staircase leading to the second floor. It was sturdy and impressive in size, easily wide enough for five people to walk abreast up and down. It reminded Bea of the staircase at her school.

While they watched, a nurse entered the hall from a room at the far end. She was guiding a wheelchair carrying a pale, thin man with a full head of bushy, white hair. His legs were wrapped in a quilt. His upper body leaned so far to one side that his head rested against the nurse's hand gripping the handle bar. Bea watched until they turned down another hallway and rolled out of sight.

"The first floor is the infirmary, for the people who need wheelchairs or can't climb the stairs," Walter offered.

"Walter, do you know anything about the nurse who lives

in the apartment across from Lila's?"

"You mean old pointy nose, pickle face Grim?"

"I guess so," Bea chuckled at Walter's description of her new neighbor. "Why would Lila say I needed to be on my best behavior when I meet her? Doesn't she like children?"

"I don't think she likes anyone. I'd rather die of appendicitis in my own bed than go to the infirmary and have her for a nurse."

Walter stepped back from the glass. "Come on, I'll show you the front entrance."

Bea followed Walter off the porch and around to the north side of the building.

Young maple trees bordered the straight, graveled driveway leading up to the farm from a paved highway in the distance. Where Walter and Bea stood, the driveway widened, encircling a cement water fountain.

The fountain was simple in design, a gray, shallow bowl, six feet in diameter, perched atop a squat, pedestal base. From a protruding pipe in the center, a continuous spray of water shot upwards, then spread and fell back into the pool of water.

Bea was immediately enchanted. Here was a water fountain like the one in the square on the street in Paris where Juliette lived.

"Oh, Walter. Look."

Water droplets pocked the surface of the pool, creating gentle ripples in the water. Bea stepped up on a cement rise at the base of the pedestal and plunged her hands into the clear, cool water. She spread her fingers, dragging her hands through the water in gentle figure-eights.

After a while Bea lifted her hands from the water, intending to pat her hot cheeks with her wet fingers. It was then, while looking through the haze of spray, that she saw the birds.

43

There were two, perched on the rim of the bowl. Bea quickly stepped around the curve of the fountain to reach them. The birds were the same gray color as the fountain. But, where the fountain had the rough form of cement, the birds were skillfully carved in stone, their surfaces smooth.

The neck of one bird was outstretched, the head lowered, as if seeking a drink of water. The other bird stood erect, it's head cocked, like a sentry on alert.

"Watch this," Walter said, stepping up beside her.

He filled his cupped hands with water and released it over the birds. Bathed in water, the birds sparkled. Their stone bodies darkened and were visibly spotted with black flecks.

Water dripped from the beak of the lowest bird and plopped onto Bea's extended finger.

"What kind of birds are they?" Bea asked.

Walter shrugged his shoulders. "No one's ever said. Maybe barn swallows. We have lots of those here. You can see their nests under the eaves of the barn."

Bea crinkled her nose, studying the birds, running her hand along their flared, tail feathers.

Nooo, she hesitated, not barn birds.

Then, lifting her chin, "They look like doves to me and they've arrived here from someplace far away. I'll name them Mr. and Mrs. Paris."

"Why Paris?"

"It's a place in France I've been reading about. They have lots of doves there."

"Seems silly to give names to stone birds. It's not like they're going anywhere and you need to call them back." Walter slapped the side of the fountain, bending over in an exaggerated motion, laughing at his own joke. Bea managed a forced grin, resigned to his lack of imagination.

"Not that you'd understand," she added, but I always give

names to things I like. At home, in our backyard, we have an apple tree I named Willow."

Walter couldn't think of a response to this news so he just said "Oh," and hopped down to the ground.

"Let's go," he said, "I still have lots to show you and there's someone I want you to meet."

"All right."

They left the graveled driveway for a softer route across the lawns, wiping their hands dry on their pants legs as they went, leaving the birds drying in the sun.

Bea never expected the County Poor Farm to look so much like a real farm. There were numerous fields, portioned into a variety of vegetable plots. Under the hot sun, men wielding hoes were scattered among the rows. A few of the plants, including lettuce, carrots and corn, Bea recognized. In some of the fields she could see both tractors and horses at work pulling farm equipment.

Bea was anxious to see the farm animals. Walter showed her the pigsty first. They walked the length of the building, right down the center, on a raised aisle overlooking adjoining pens on either side. In each pen, there was a wood trough. Walter explained to Bea how food was brought into the building in wheelbarrows and dumped into the troughs from above.

The pigsty was dimly lit through high, narrow windows and the air had the heavy, cloying odor of wet earth and rotten food scraps. Once outside, Bea took a grateful breath of fresh air.

Walter pointed out the ice storage shed, the laundry, the greenhouse, the boiler room, the incinerator and the water tower.

"You'll never guess what this is," Walter said, stopping in front of a square, wood plank building near the water tower.

The building was small, almost like a child's cottage. Bea walked around its perimeter, stopping to peer into windows at the front and back, but she was unable to see beyond the closed blinds.

"I give up," she admitted. "What is it?"

Walter answered in a solemn, yet bemused voice. "It's the morgue."

To Walter's satisfaction Bea was obligingly startled and jumped back from the building, jerking her hand from where she'd left it resting on the windowpane.

"Really?" she asked, her eyes widened. "Is there, wellll," she paused, "anyone inside?"

"Not now. But when someone dies, they keep the body in there until the coroner can come out from Portland and get it."

"Gee," was all she could think to say.

Moving away from the morgue, they approached three sheds enclosed in wire mesh fencing. Home to the farm's chickens.

Bea lifted a white feather from where it had caught in the fence. She held it lightly by the quill and then puckered her lips and blew it gently from her grasp. It drifted toward the ground in a careless path and landed on the toe of her shoe. Picking it up, she put it in her pocket.

"The dairy barn is my favorite place," Walter said, turning and walking away, "That's why I saved it for last."

The dairy barn was the largest of all the farm buildings and the farthest south. It was red with a gray, arched roof. Walter and Bea scrambled over a gate and started across a pasture in that direction. About fifty yards from the gate, a loosely bunched herd of tan colored Jersey cows were grazing. One cow, feeding at the outer edge of the herd, looked up as they neared and took several hesitant steps in their direction.

Bea quickly realized that having seen a cow in a book, or

even in a pen at the state fair, wasn't anything like meeting one face-to-face in an open field. She was embarrassed to let-on she was afraid, but couldn't resist stepping around Walter, leaving him between her and the approaching cow. They kept walking and so did the cow.

"Those cows won't hurt you. They're just curious," was all Walter said. Bea had expected him to tease her and was relieved when he didn't.

Approaching the barn, Bea looked back over her shoulder; the curious cow had turned back toward the herd and resumed grazing.

Walter hurried the last few steps to the barn door. After he lifted a wood bar, the lower half of the door swung open and he ducked inside. Bea ducked in after him.

In contrast to the pigsty, the barn had a pleasant smell and feel. Overriding the presence of animals were the warm, dry aromas of hay and grain.

Bea found herself standing at one end of a long, rectangular room. Walter explained that the metal bars Bea saw lined up on both sides of the room were milking stanchions.

"Cows put their heads between the bars to reach the grain they eat while they're milked. The cows even know which stanchion is their own and walk to the right one every time they're milked."

Just like a family at dinner, Bea thought. For a brief moment she envisioned her dad, and mom, and Billy, and herself, at their usual places around the dinner table.

To Bea's relief the stanchions were empty. There wasn't a cow in sight, only a man wearing a flannel shirt, blue jeans and knee high rubber boots. He was spraying water from a hose, forcing bits of hay and manure into a shallow ditch in the cement floor.

"Hey," Walter called. The man looked in their direction

and raised one arm. "I'll be finished in a minute," he called back in a kind voice, and resumed spraying.

Walter sat down on an overturned bucket to wait, and Bea leaned against the doorframe.

Walter said, "I bet you didn't know these cows supply all the milk for the county prison."

"You mean there's a prison here too?"

"Not here exactly. But it's only a half-mile down the road. If it wasn't for all the trees, you could probably see it. One time I rode along in the truck making the milk delivery."

The mention of a prison reminded Bea of headlines she'd noticed in the newspaper last winter.

"Isn't the county prison where those two brothers were sent after they were caught robbing banks in Portland?"

"Yep, the Grimsby brothers. One of them works in the prison kitchen. Jiggs told me when I helped him unload the milk."

"Who is Jiggs?"

"That's me." The man with the hose stepped up next to Walter and slapped him playfully on the shoulder. He grinned over at Bea. "You must be Lila's guest."

"I'm Bea."

"Well, glad to meet you. Don't let this Walter sprout fool you. He only knows half of what he says."

Walter's face flushed and he playfully knocked Jiggs' hand off his shoulder.

"I'm just showing Bea around," Walter said, "My mother made me."

Jiggs lifted the hose he'd carried with him, and had been slowly coiling, onto his shoulder. "You two have a good time. I need to get back to work."

"See you later," said Walter.

"Bye," Bea said.

On the return trip across the pasture, Bea was relieved to see the cows had wandered out of sight.

They were scaling the gate when Walter said, "Jiggs used to be a clown, in a real circus. You should see how good he juggles."

"Why isn't he a clown now?"

"Because people couldn't afford to buy tickets. His circus closed, so he found a job floating logs down the Sandy River. Then, one day last summer, he fell between two logs and crushed his legs. He had no place to go, so he came here while his legs were healing. He still limps some."

"Are you ready to go see Lila's office?"

Bea only nodded. Her stomach had begun to growl and she wondered where she would eat lunch.

Bea was suddenly very, very tired. And while her steps matched Walter's, she felt alone, overwhelmed by a place she couldn't have imagined only a week before.

CHAPTER

6

Morning sounds drifted in through the loft windows on Bea's second day at the Poor Farm. She lay awake, listening.

She recognized Mr. Briggs' voice in a conversation with another man on the front porch below. In the distance, there were shouts she couldn't identify, a door slammed, dropped pails collided with a metallic clang.

Wheels crunched over gravel as a vehicle descended the driveway. Bea wondered if Jiggs was setting out on the daily milk delivery to the prison.

Today is Saturday, Bea remembered, enjoying the luxury of sleeping in. The clock on the bedside table read 9:00 a.m. In a dreamy mood, Bea stared at the ceiling and thought back over her first week at the farm.

Monday morning, she'd risen early to join Lila for breakfast. Afterward, they'd walked the short distance to the two story building referred to as "The Laundry", where Lila had a sunny corner office on the first floor. The Laundry was connected by covered walkways to the larger dormitory, so the entire structure formed an 'L'. Bea had learned she could help out in the laundry during the week.

Most of the other laundry workers were women who lived at the farm. The older ladies were friendly, if somewhat slow workers, and they had all welcomed Bea. One woman remarked that Bea's youthful energy would provide a real spark to their group.

In the loft, the sounds of activity coming up from the kitchen below intruded into Bea's thoughts. She scooted out of bed. Her stomach began to growl as she pulled on her dress and stuffed her pajamas under the bed pillow.

Bea's feet fairly flew down the stairs. Anyone watching would be hard pressed to recognize this girl as the one who'd timidly climbed to the loft for the first time only seven days before.

"Morning, Lila," Bea called into the kitchen from the bottom of the staircase.

"Morning, Dear," came faintly back to Bea as she scooted into the bathroom and closed the door.

When she emerged a few minutes later, her tousled hair was smooth and bore damp tracks from the hairbrush she'd wet under the faucet.

A box of Post Toasties sat on the table. Bea fetched a bowl and milk from the cooler. Lila had eaten earlier and was now busy mixing up a batch of mayonnaise. Bea recognized the sharp aroma of vinegar.

While Bea ate, she watched Lila adding oil, eggs and sugar to the dab of vinegar already measured and poured into a white crock with a blue stripe around the rim. Lila held the crock snugly against her soft, ample waist and began vigorously whipping the mixture with a wooden spoon. Bea finished her cereal.

"Before I do anything else, I'm going to write a letter to Mom," Bea told Lila, while she washed her bowl and put away the milk.

"Be sure to send my love," Lila replied. "Oh, and tell your mom I said that that little girl of hers is quite a handful, but she'll do in a pinch." Lila winked at Bea and her face wore a teasing grin. Bea blushed and shifted her feet, feeling awkward, but secretly warmed by Lila's show of affection.

Bea left the kitchen, and Lila, after switching the spoon to her other hand, continued beating the mayonnaise.

In the loft, Bea sat at the desk to write her first letter to her mother. That last night at home, while lying in bed, she had promised herself to write cheerful letters, no matter how awful things might be.

Bea's neat, rounded script soon filled several pages with entertaining descriptions of the farm, its people and animals.

She didn't seem to notice how easily and happily the lines filled the page.

By late morning, her letter finished and addressed, Bea sat cross-legged on the floor of the landing outside Lila's apartment. In her right hand she held a small rubber ball. Scattered on the floor in front of her, like small, pointy stars, were ten jacks. The jacks were worn, with only a few remaining flecks of their original silver paint. Bea was happily engaged in a game of "Jacks", pleased to be on her "foursies" after only dropping the ball once.

Bea studied the positions of the jacks spread out on the floor, planning her next move. After several false starts, she tossed the ball overhead and quickly scooped up four jacks. Then, flipping her hand palm side up, while keeping a secure hold on the jacks, she caught the ball on the first bounce.

Bea set the captured jacks to the side. There were six left. She was planning her next move when she heard a faint squeak, immediately followed by a soft step. A pair of shoes appeared on the floor among the jacks. The leather shoes were white, with thick soles, rounded toes and tight laces. Nurse shoes.

Bea was finally meeting the mysterious Miss Grim. And in a manner she'd never expected, from the bottom up.

With a great deal of trepidation Bea lifted her gaze past the pair of knobby ankles and thin lower legs covered in white, cotton stockings that disappeared underneath a white nursing uniform. The skirt hung in sharp, starchy folds below a flat bodice with its row of buttons and stiff pointed collar.

Bea's eyes were shiny with apprehension when she finally looked directly into Miss Grim's face.

Miss Grim had steely grey eyes that were streaked with yellow, like a cat's eyes Bea thought, and set close to the bridge of her long, sharp nose. Her thin, frizzy brown hair was held back from her high, pale forehead with bobby pins and tucked underneath her nurse's cap.

The look she gave Bea was cold and piercing, and held the kind of intensity that caused any child under their scrutiny to squirm with unacknowledged guilt. Bea shifted her focus to a twitch near Miss Grim's left eye.

"Hello, Miss Grim," Bea managed to say, her voice coming out in a nervous squeak.

"Hello, you must be Lila's girl."

"Yes, I'm Bea."

"I supposed you were somebody. Bea's as good as anything," Miss Grim replied. Then she took a deep breath and in a flat, almost apologetic voice that conveyed little genuine concern, said, "I'm sorry to hear of your poor family's difficulties. I hope your mother will be well soon."

Bea nodded, and managed a quiet, "Thank you."

"You'll do well," Miss Grim continued, "while you reside in this home to be on your best behavior. Please remember that I won't tolerate noisy children who leave their toys lying around for me to trip over."

"Yes, Ma'am. I was just putting them away."

Bea anxiously bent down and retrieved a cloth drawstring bag from her dress pocket. She quickly scooped the remaining jacks into the bag, all the while feeling the weight of Miss Grim's disapproval settling over her head.

After taking a moment to push her wire-rimmed glasses back from tip of her nose, Miss Grim stepped past Bea and continued downstairs.

That's when Bea noticed the nurse's injured hand. The skin on the back of her right hand and wrist was puckered with white shiny patches, evidence left from a serious burn sometime in her past. In her other hand she carried a letter. The envelope was turned so that Bea couldn't read the address on the front.

Seeing the envelope gave Bea a start. She realized Miss Grim could possibly have been writing a letter to her own mother at the same time Bea was writing hers. Bea tried to imagine Miss Grim as a baby, her stern, sharp-nosed face scowling out at the world from inside the folds of a baby blanket. The image made Bea giggle. But, her enjoyment was to be short lived.

She closed the bag of jacks, pulling the strings taut. As she scrambled to her feet, the rubber ball slipped from her fingers. She gasped and then watched in disbelief as the ball bounced once on the landing and then shot toward the staircase.

In perfect arcs, it bounced from one step to another, all the way to the bottom of the staircase, where it rolled across the floor and finally came to rest against the heel of Miss Grim's shoe.

Bea's stomach rolled with each bounce of the descending ball.

Bea clung to the newel post and watched, her legs turned weak and rubbery with disbelief and fear. Then, unbelievably, Bea was saved by the appearance of an unlikely hero, Walter.

At just that moment, he burst through the front door.

"Bea," he yelled urgently, when he saw her standing at the top of the staircase, "There's some guy wants to see you."

"Oh, it must be Billy. Is it Billy?"

"Got me. Whoever he is, he sent me to tell you to come outside."

The errant ball forgotten, Bea hurried down the stairs and followed Walter outside. Only later did she realize his interruption had allowed her to slip past Miss Grim and escape a good scolding, if not something much worse.

Outside on the front lawn, Walter pointed in the direction of the maple trees bordering the long front driveway. At the far end of the row of trees, almost to the highway, a lone figure could be seen under a tree, leaning against the trunk.

Bea cupped a hand to her mouth, shouted Billy's name and waved her arm. The person leaning against the tree straightened and returned the wave.

Bea rushed from the yard and down the driveway with Walter close at her heels. The loose gravel slipped noisily beneath their feet. Bea's heart was pounding when she pulled up beside Billy.

"Why are you waiting out here?" she asked. "Come on up to the house."

"Billy didn't answer immediately, or in the manner Bea expected. Instead, he shifted his feet and fiddled with the collar on his shirt, hesitating. Finally, his words came out in a rush, "Bea, I'm not coming any farther because I'm not going to stay here."

For a moment Bea stared silently at Billy, trying to take in what he'd just said.

"You have to stay," she said indignantly, "Dad said so."

"Things have changed, Bea. While I was at Bob's, his dad brought home a bulletin announcing able-bodied workers

56

were needed in the fruit orchards in Wenatchee, Washington. Bob's older brother Jack decided to go there. He said Bob and I could join him."

"But…" Bea could only stutter.

"Bob's father called Dad and asked for his permission Bea. Dad said I could go."

Billy reached into his blue jeans pocket and pulled out a piece of smudged paper that had been carefully folded into a tight square.

"I wrote this note to Mom. Will you send it for me?" Bea slowly reached out and took it from his outstretched hand.

Now that he'd delivered his news, Billy's spirits visibly lifted and his manner turned jovial.

"You're doing all right aren't you? Is Lila as nice as Mom said?"

"Yeah, she's nice. And I have my own bedroom in a loft."

"That's great, Bea. See, you'll be fine without me around. Besides, I'll probably make so much money I'll be able to bring home presents for everyone. Then you will be glad I didn't stay."

Billy cocked his head in the direction of the highway.

For the first time, Bea noticed the car parked at the edge of the road. She recognized Jack and Bob inside the cab. Bob stuck his arm out the passenger window and waved.

"I need to leave, Bea," Billy said. The guys are waiting for me."

Tears burned hot in Bea's eyes, and she impulsively wrapped her arms around her brother. Billy's neck and face flushed pink.

"No need to squish a fella. Summer will be over before you know it. See ya," he said.

Bea stepped back. "See ya," she answered.

Bea watched Billy until he'd climbed inside the car next

to Bob and the car eased back onto the highway, headed east.

During the meeting between Bea and Billy, Walter waited on the driveway a short distance back, curious, but not sure if he should intrude. He tried not to look in their direction and kept himself busy picking up small rocks with his bare toes. Occasionally, he bent down in search of the perfect stone to throw at a passing bird.

Bea wiped at her eyes with the back of her hand and headed back up the driveway. Walter fell into step beside her. Rather than returning to the house they turned at the top of the drive and headed toward the water fountain.

Bea stood on the fountain's ledge and patted the stone heads of Mr. and Mrs. Paris. Mrs. Paris wore a daisy chain necklace that Bea had made for her earlier in the week. Now the stems were limp and the edges of the white petals were curled and brown. Bea lifted off the necklace and dropped it into the pool of water.

Walter waited across the fountain from Bea, dunking his hand into the water and then lifting it out and watching the water drip off the ends of his fingertips.

"I'm sorry about your brother," he said.

Bea bit her lip and didn't look up. They both watched the necklace slowly sink below the surface.

Walter paced, circling the fountain. "If I had a brother, I'd be glad he was going away if he brought me presents."

"Well, he's not your brother, all right," Bea snapped, glaring up at Walter. Her angry words had a bitter taste and she knew they were unfair. Walter had only meant to make her feel better.

Not quite willing to apologize, she gentled her voice instead and said, "I need to take this note to the house and tell Lila about Billy. Do you want to come?"

Walter shrugged his shoulders and mumbled, "Yeah, sure."

The first person they saw when they entered the house was Mrs. Briggs, standing upstairs on the second floor landing, talking with Lila.

Bea and Walter crouched unnoticed at the bottom of the staircase to listen.

"I can't understand how it could just disappear. I'm sure it was hanging in its usual place yesterday," Mrs. Briggs said.

"Yes, I know it was," Lila answered, "I clearly remember glancing at it when I left the house in the morning. Maybe someone in the dormitory borrowed it?"

"If they did, they certainly didn't ask me," replied a disgruntled Mrs. Briggs. "No, there is definitely something going on here. Last week my Henry went out on the front porch after dinner to smoke his pipe. A short while later he came inside for a drink of water, leaving his pipe on the arm of the chair. But when he returned to the porch, his pipe was gone. It was a very expensive pipe too. Last years Christmas present," she added indignantly.

Briggs shifted into a more relaxed stance and chuckled. "To tell you the truth, I thought maybe Henry lost it himself and just didn't want to admit to it. But now, with the clock disappearing too, I'm afraid we have a thief."

"A thief?" Walter and Bea silently mouthed the words and resumed listening with renewed interest.

"Oh surely not," Lila said. "There must be a logical explanation."

"I know you like to think the best of people Lila, but until we know the truth we all better keep a close eye on things."

"Thank you for letting me know," Lila said.

"I don't know what this world's coming to," Walter's mother muttered as she said her good-byes to Lila and started down the steps.

Walter and Bea were quickly on their feet, their faces

turned upwards toward Mrs. Briggs with looks of complete innocence.

They had been so caught up in eavesdropping that they hadn't noticed someone entering the house after them. They both jumped in surprise when Miss Grim's voice spoke sharply behind them.

"Can't you children remember to close a door?"

"Oh, Virginia," Mrs. Briggs said, pausing on the bottom step, "there's something I wanted to discuss with..." Her words trailed off into silence when Miss Grim appeared not to hear and hurried past them up the stairs. The three left standing at the bottom of the staircase watched her hasty retreat until she reached the door of her apartment, turned the key in the lock, and disappeared inside.

Mrs. Briggs shrugged her shoulders.

"Walter, I want you to come inside now."

"I'll be there in a minute, Mom."

"See that you are."

Walter waited until she left before he leaned toward Bea with a secretive air.

"It's her. I know it's her," he said.

"It's what? I mean, it's her, who?" Bea whispered back.

"Miss Grim, she's the thief. Anyone that mean has to be hiding something."

"Lila says she only acts mean because she's lonely."

"Lila's not a detective. She doesn't understand about this kind of stuff."

"And you do?" Bea asked doubtfully.

"I read *Dick Tracy* and *Orphan Annie*, and I know what real criminals act like."

"The comics aren't real Walter."

"They're just as real as that lady detective, Juliette, you're always talking about."

60

"Suppose you are right. Shouldn't we tell someone?"

"Who'd believe us, we're kids. We need proof. We'll have to come up with a plan to spy on her, try to catch her in the act."

Bea nodded in agreement.

"Then they'd have to believe us," she said.

"Right. I better get inside. Remember, this is our secret."

Bea climbed the stairs. Her thoughts turned inward. She hadn't wanted to come to the farm. She'd been sure God had made a big mistake, or at the very least didn't consider the concerns of one twelve-year-old girl of much importance. Was her mom right when she said that when disappointments come that only means God had a better plan.

So far, living at the poor farm hadn't really turned out so bad. She'd daydreamed often enough in the past about one day being a detective, and now there was a thief in their midst. She and Walter had been handed an actual, bona fide case. Maybe daydreams and prayers weren't altogether different.

Reaching for the apartment door she was reminded of the paper she carried in her hand, Billy's letter to Mom.

Even Billy had deserted her.

CHAPTER
7

More than two weeks had passed since Billy's brief visit to the farm.

Soft blowing afternoon breezes moved through the open second story windows on the drying floor of the laundry building, a place where clotheslines in close, parallel rows, spanned the length of the room between the north and south facing walls.

Bea had nearly finished her last chore for the day. She reached into a wheeled cart and lifted out the remaining wet bedsheet. She tossed one end of the sheet over the stiff cotton cord and secured it with a wooden clothespin. Moving down the line, she stretched out the sheet and clipped on the final clothespin.

"Finished," she said out loud, dropping her weary arms to her sides with a sigh of relief.

Bea pushed the emptied cart to the end of the line and parked it near a small service elevator at the top of the stairs leading up from the first floor. The elevator brought the canvas bags of wet, clean linens up from the first floor wash room. After they were dry and folded the linens were returned on the same elevator and stored for use in the dormitory and kitchen.

"Bye, see you tomorrow," Bea called to her boss, a woman named Bell, who was standing at a near-by table folding tablecloths.

Not waiting for a reply, Bea bolted down the stairs to the first floor. She hop-scotched her way down the first floor hall by only stepping on the red linoleum squares and avoiding the black ones. Just as she left the building, Walter ran past.

"Come on," he yelled, without even slowing down or looking to see if she would follow.

Bea immediately forgot her weariness and raced after Walter. She finally caught up to him at the back of a shed housing farm equipment.

Many years ago, a broken-down wagon had been pushed up against the back wall of the shed and abandoned. Over time a neglected tangle of grass and weeds and wild blackberry vines had twined through the spokes of its wheels and climbed up and over the rough wood sides of the wagon. Now the wagon was almost entirely hidden inside this growing green shroud.

Walter wasn't alone behind the shed. A team of horses was harnessed and standing in front of the wagon, facing away. Jiggs stood at the horse's heads. He had a firm grasp on their halters where they passed beneath their chins. At the horse's rear, a chain was attached to the wood bar on the harness called the "double tree" and strung out in the grass.

A second man was bent over securing the trailing end of the chain to the wagon tongue he'd pried out of the thick grass. He gave the chain a tug before he stood and yelled, "Ready."

Bea turned to Walter, "What are they doing?"

"Shh, just watch!" he replied curtly.

Bea figured Walter didn't know what was happening any more than she did. She moved toward Jiggs, intending to ask him, but he waved her back. Bea crossed her arms in front of her chest and waited.

Jiggs clicked his tongue and tugged on the halters.

"Step out girls," he beckoned.

The horse on Jiggs' left tossed her head and snorted, flinging wet green globs onto Jiggs' shoulder. Finally, as if in unspoken agreement, both horses lowered their heads and leaned forward into their wide, powerful chests. Their front legs shifted then settled. The chain lifted from the grass and stretched taut.

"Pull," Bea encouraged, lifting up on to her toes. "You can do it."

The wagon slowly began to roll forward, emitting creaks and snaps and eerie screeches and raising quite a racket.

"Ouch," Bea covered her ears, grimacing.

Walter "Whooped".

The wagon was eventually dragged into the clear.

After the men and horses left with the tottering wagon, Walter and Bea stepped over to the mound of briars and peered into the open space created by the departed wagon.

"It's like a cave," Bea exclaimed.

Walter knelt down and crawled inside. Broken bits of prickly vine were scattered on the ground and dangled over his head, catching in his hair.

Walter backed out, dragging bits of debris with him. He stood up and swiped at his pant legs, very gingerly picking off a thorny stick embedded in his sock.

Bea pointed to Walter's hand.

"You're bleeding," she said.

He glanced at his hand and then wiped it on the front of his shirt before licking his palm.

"Yuck," Bea grimaced.

Walter seemed unfazed; in fact his face gleamed like a pirate who's found buried treasure.

"If we cleared out these broken vines," Walter said, now drying his hand on his shirt, "we could use this place for a clubhouse."

Bea was immediately caught up with the idea.

"It could be both a clubhouse, and the office for our detective agency. We'll need to lay something on the ground to make a soft floor," she said, her head quickly filling with ideas. "And we could use apple crates for shelves; and I could ask Lila for a sheet to hang up for a door; and…"

Walter didn't wait to hear the rest. "I'll run home and get a rake and Mom's rose clippers," he said, setting off for the house.

"I'll get some cardboard boxes from the kitchen," she hollered at his fleeting back.

Bea returned to the clubhouse carrying a tall stack of cardboard boxes. Words printed on the sides of the boxes advertised Babbitt's Cleanser, and Edward's Coffee, plain or drip.

With the boxes blocking her forward view, Bea had been forced to navigate the whole way from the kitchen by looking at the ground between her feet. A short distance from the clubhouse the box on the top of the stack fell. She kicked it ahead of her the last few yards.

Bea glanced over her shoulder toward the house. There was no sign yet of Walter.

She knelt down and set to work on the boxes. With a great deal of grunting and tugging she managed to pull apart the overlapping flaps on the bottom of each box, collapsing it. She piled the boxes on the ground before flopping down on top of the pile to flatten them farther, and wait for Walter's return.

It wasn't long before Walter came huffing and puffing around the corner of the shed. His cheeks were red from exertion and the ends of his blonde hair were dark with sweat. He carried a rake and clippers and dropped them on the grass.

"You got em." Bea said, sitting up.

"That's not all I got. I got something even more important.

"What? I don't see anything."

"It's in my pocket. It's a clue. At least I think it's a clue."

"You mean a clue to prove Miss Grim is a thief?"

Bea could hardly contain her excitement. From the time she and Walter had made their pact to spy on Miss Grim and find the proof they needed to convince the adults that she was the mysterious thief, Bea and Walter had failed to catch her filling her pockets with anything more sinister than crumpled handkerchiefs.

Walter pulled something yellow from his shirt pocket and handed it to Bea.

She found herself holding a piece of stiff, rectangular shaped paper. At first glance, Bea thought it was a movie ticket, until she read the words printed on one side.

Stone's Pawnshop
103 6th Ave., Portland, Ore.
Account number: 1405
Receipt for items #106, #107

"It's a ticket from a pawnshop," Bea said, glancing up at Walter.

Walter looked puzzled. "What's a pawnshop?"

"It's a place where people take valuable items to exchange for cash. The pawnshop keeps whatever's brought in for 30 days. If the original owner can get enough money before the thirty days pass, he can return and buy back his stuff. After thirty days, the owner of the shop can sell it to someone else.

"How do you know about pawnshops?" Walter asked, reluctant to admit a girl, six months his junior, could possibly know something he didn't.

"I know about pawnshops," Bea explained with a certain amount of exasperation, "because one time last winter I was helping my dad at our grocery store when this man came in. He seemed real sad and discouraged.

"I heard him tell my dad that he'd been searching for a month and couldn't find a steady job. When he couldn't make his house payment and buy food, he'd been forced to take some of his wife's wedding silver to a pawnshop. He told my dad he was praying hard for a good job so he'd be able to earn enough money to return for the silver before it was too late."

"Wow! Then this piece of paper really is a clue," Walter said with pride.

"A clue?" Bea was puzzled.

"Yeah, don't you see. This is a receipt for two items. And we know two items disappeared: the pipe and the clock. Miss Grim must have stolen them and then sold them to the pawn shop for money."

"How do you know this ticket belongs to Miss Grim?"

"Oh, I haven't told you the best part.

"When I asked Mom for the garden tools, she said the clippers and the rake were both out in the garage. I found them all right and was starting back here when Miss Grim drove up. I stayed and watched while she parked her car and got out. What she didn't notice, but I did, was this piece of yellow paper. It fell out of her car when she opened the door to get out.

"My detective instincts just took over," Walter bragged.

"I quickly walked up to the car and covered the paper with my foot.

"I knew she'd probably yell at me for standing there so I said, "Miss Grim, let me close the car door for you".

"Boy oh boy, you should have seen the look on her face. It was sooo funny."

Bea shrieked with laughter.

"So, what did she do?"

Before he answered, Walter pulled himself up straight and drew his face into a pinched imitation of Miss Grim's. In a high whiny voice he answered.

"'I'm happy to see you're adopting a gentleman's ways Walter. I must say, up until now I haven't held out much hope for you.'"

Walter barely managed to get through his speech before collapsing on the ground, rolling about on the grass in open-mouthed laughter. Sprawled on the cardboard pile, Bea laughed hysterically until her sides hurt and her stomach began quivering.

After catching her breath, Bea sat up and turned to Walter. Mimicking his earlier imitation of Miss Grim, she squealed, "I just have no hope for you, Walter."

This bit of acting set off another round of laughter.

When they were finally spent and quiet Walter got to his feet.

"I meant to tell you, I can't work on the clubhouse anymore today." Walter said. I have to help with the evening milking. Mom's fixing something for me to eat right now."

Walter gathered the tools he'd dropped on the grass earlier and shoved them into the opened space under the vines. Together, Bea and Walter tossed the boxes in as well.

"I'll find something to keep the ticket in, in case we need it for evidence," Bea said, tucking it into her pocket, and feeling very much like her heroine, Juliette, would approve.

"Walter, I think our luck is changing. Now we have a clubhouse and our first bit of real evidence."

"You're right. We need a name, something official." Walter scrunched his eyes while slowly tapping his forehead with one hand in deep concentration. "I think I'll make a sign that says, W & B Detective Agency."

Bea thought B & W Detective Agency sounded better, but decided not to argue since she got to keep the clues.

Together they headed back to the house. Bea didn't know about Walter, but she was already making plans to decorate her half of the clubhouse.

CHAPTER 8

L ila plopped the silverware into the kitchen sink before glancing at Bea, who lingered nearby, leaning against the refrigerator. "Shoo," Lila ordered, "Go on outside and wait, I move even slower with you pestering me to hurry." She lifted one hand from the pan of soapy dishwater and fluttered her fingers, sending a wet spray toward Bea.

"Oh, all right," Bea relented, snatching the last piece of bacon off the platter on her way out.

Today was the Fourth of July. Everyone who lived at the farm had been looking forward to the picnic planned for that afternoon in the shady grove of oak trees next to the dormitory. Lila had been put in charge of arranging the outside tables and decorations. Bea had been awake and eager to help with the decorations since early that morning.

In the front yard, Bea stood by the front gate under the trellis. The hop plants, only small mounds at the base of the trellis when she first arrived at the farm, had flourished into lush vines that climbed the trellis sides and spread over its arched top. Bea searched hopefully amongst the leaves and stems, but didn't see any signs of the fragile blooms her father had told her about.

She pushed through the gate, wondering if she had time to run down to the new clubhouse. After wasting one entire afternoon last week arguing with Walter about how they would arrange their stuff inside it, they'd finally agreed on an imaginary line that divided the space right down the middle, giving each one total control over their own half of the clubhouse.

Deciding to wait, Bea continued with light, eager steps, past the fountain and the north end of the dormitory to its east-side porch. Happily, she spotted one rocking chair not already occupied. Bea crossed the porch and sat down. With a push of her foot she set her chair in motion, joining the seesaw rhythm of the other rockers.

To Bea's right, sat a tiny woman whose snappy, blue eyes peered out curiously from a worn and wrinkled face. She grinned up at Bea, revealing a slice of gray gums and one yellowed tooth, set loose in her bottom jaw. Because her feet hung several inches above the floor, she kept her chair in motion by repeatedly bobbing her head.

On Bea's other side, the man with the long beard, who had ridden on the trolley with Bea and her father, was asleep. Bea had learned his name was Ed. Occasionally, he muttered, or blew out a deep rush of breath that ruffled his lips.

Bea closed her eyes, maintaining the motion of her chair, while in her mind she returned to the puzzle of the stolen clock and pipe, and the recovered pawn ticket. She was keeping the ticket inside an empty cigar box at the club-house. Bea tried not to be discouraged by the lack of any new clues. After all, Bea reminded herself, it had taken Juliette one whole winter to solve the case of the missing gardener.

Bea remembered her father saying that if a person wasn't caught in wrongdoing, and punished, they were sure to try it again. If that was true, and Miss Grim was the thief, then

Bea was determined to catch her.

When Lila, together with Walter, finally appeared, Bea joined them on the lawn.

"Go ahead, open 'em," Lila urged, pointing to a group of boxes that had earlier been carried up from the dormitory basement by two of the men residents and left there.

Walter quickly dropped to the ground, scrambling to get the first box open before Bea. Bea 'oohed' and 'aahed' as each lid was removed and the contents revealed.

Rolls of red, white and blue streamers, small silky American flags glued to gold painted sticks with pointy tops, shiny silver tassels, candles, and paper stars and flowers.

While Lila was helping Bea sort the decorations, Jiggs arrived riding high on the drivers seat of a flatbed wagon pulled by the mare he'd named Eleanor, in honor of the President's wife. The many years Jiggs had performed and traveled with the circus had fostered his love of animals; a love which he now poured out on all the farm animals, although Eleanor was his favorite.

Unlike most people in the progressive 1930's, Jiggs felt a tug of regret over the change from 'horsepower' to the newer gasoline driven engines. He had a real fondness and respect for workhorses.

"You can give those mechanical contraptions names, alright," he always said, "but you can't give them a soul."

When Walter saw the wagon arrive, he lost interest in the boxes. "I saw all these decorations last year," he said. He took off across the lawn to join Jiggs.

While the men unloaded sawhorses and boards from the wagon bed, Lila sorted the decorations and together with Bea, carried them across the yard to the porch.

"I need to check on preparations in the kitchen," Lila told Bea. "Think you can handle decorating the porch by your self?"

Bea eagerly set to work, helped along with smiles of encouragement and suggestions from the "porchsitters".

When she'd finished, Bea stood back on the lawn and viewed the now festive porch, while absently sucking a sore spot that had developed on her thumb from tacking up the decorations.

Bea felt proud and pleased with the results. She scooped up a handful of American flags and returned to the porch, intent on giving a flag to each person there. Ed was still asleep, his hands resting in his lap. With great care, Bea inserted a flag between his curled fingers. She muffled the sound of her giggles behind her hand as she quietly backed off the porch.

Eleanor was still hitched to the wagon, so Bea started across the lawn to visit her.

"Hi, Eleanor, sweet girl," she crooned.

Eleanor lowered her nose into Bea's open palm, snorting and sniffing for food, tickling Bea's hand.

"I like you too," Bea chuckled, while reaching up to smooth the tuft of mane that fell between Eleanor's ears, covering her forehead.

"Isn't this just the greatest day," Bea said aloud, enjoying the sound of the words. Eleanor snickered.

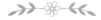

Walter rose from his chair. "I'm getting another piece of cake," he said, before striding off toward the dessert table. In the chair next to his, Bea stretched her legs and crossed her hands over her rounded stomach. How can he possibly eat another bite, she wondered.

Bea looked out across the picnic area. She'd never seen so many of the farm's residents in one place at the same time.

Even the people confined to wheelchairs were outside on the lawn. Everyone was enjoying the holiday, the change in routine.

A few hours earlier, the picnic tables Jiggs and Walter had erected with saw horses and boards had been weighted down with platters of fried chicken and bowls of baked beans, potato salad, sliced tomatoes, green beans, and desserts. Now almost all the platters were empty.

Bea watched Walter approach the dessert table and grab one of the last remaining pieces of chocolate cake.

In a shady spot beneath a large oak tree, Lila was sitting with Mr. and Mrs. Briggs and Miss Grim. Mr. Briggs was napping with his hat pulled down over his face. Lila was talking to Mrs. Briggs, who was fanning her face with a piece of folded newspaper. While Bea watched, Miss Grim dug into her pocket for a handkerchief and patted her forehead and upper lip.

The sounds of Jiggs' voice, nearby, caught Bea's attention.

"Come on fellas." He was directing his words to a group of men comfortably sprawled on blankets on the grass, enjoying their leisure. "Cows can't wait to be milked, even on the fourth of July."

Reluctantly, the men got to their feet and walked off after Jiggs, headed for the barn.

What Bea saw, or rather didn't see, when she looked back at the group under the oak tree, made her jerk upright in her seat; the chair next to Lila, where Miss Grim had been sitting, was empty.

Bea bolted up, looking in all directions until she finally caught a brief glimpse of Miss Grim's backside disappearing around the corner of the dormitory.

At that moment Walter returned.

Bea knew there wasn't time to explain.

"Walter, come on. We have to follow Miss Grim."

"Wait, I have to eat my cake."

"There isn't time. We've got to go. Now! Or we'll lose her."

Bea pulled on Walter's arm to get him moving. The piece of cake he was holding flew up out of his hand, and into the air. "Hey," Walter yelled, while diving forward with his arm stretched out. The cake landed softly on his fingertips, frosted side down. Walter closed his hand around the cake and chased after Bea.

Once past the dormitory, they knelt out of sight behind a row of rhododendrons. Walter, not wanting to chance another mishap, immediately began stuffing the entire piece of cake into his mouth. Bea peered through an opening in the branches hoping to spot Miss Grim. She may only be going back to the house, Bea realized, but she couldn't shake the feeling that Miss Grim had left the picnic with something more sinister in mind.

Then she saw her, to the left and across the clearing, standing in front of the laundry building where Bea worked; she was inserting a key into the front door lock. Before opening the door, Miss Grim swiveled her head, looking in all directions. Bea ducked out of sight.

After a few seconds, Bea peeked out again and was just in time to see Miss Grim disappear inside the building and close the door.

Bea motioned to Walter, "Come on, Miss Grim just went inside the laundry."

When Walter didn't move to follow her, Bea stopped and looked back. Walter was standing kind of hunched over and staring back at her with wide watery eyes that were almost surely beginning to bulge. In spite of his summer tan, Bea could see red splotches spreading across his cheeks. He tried to speak, but his voice came out sounding thick and mushy.

Bits of cake and drool sprayed out from between his lips.

"Yuck," Bea grimaced, leaning back.

"Swallow, Walter."

Walter stuck out his chin and gulped and gulped in an effort to get down the sticky mass of cake.

"Go," he was finally able to gasp, followed by what Bea thought was either a grunt or a word that sounded like "drink."

"Later," Bea replied hastily, relieved to see his eyes drawn back into his head and his face returning to its normal color.

They ran toward the laundry.

Walter tried the doorknob and grinned with relief to find it still unlocked. He eased the door open and they slipped inside.

While they waited for their eyes to adjust to the indoor lighting, they heard footsteps moving farther back into the building.

Walter started in the direction of the noise, with Bea following close behind. On tiptoes they moved down the hall past closed doors leading to offices and closets. For once Bea completely forgot to stay on the red squares.

They stopped just outside the open door leading into the wash room, where piles of soiled linens were loaded into machines and washed, before being sent upstairs to the drying floor. Bea and Walter held their breath and listened.

In a back area of the room someone was descending a staircase. When the sound of the footsteps faded away, they cautiously entered the wash room.

"What's downstairs?" Walter whispered to Bea.

"Just a room where donated clothes and blankets are kept. That's all."

"Do pawn shops buy clothes or blankets?" Walter asked.

"Maybe."

"If we try to follow her downstairs, she'll hear us," he said. His voice was raspy, not yet recovered.

Positive that Miss Grim was up to no good and not willing to give up the chase, Bea tried to imagine what Juliette would do in her place. Then, she had her answer.

"Walter, we don't need to follow her. That staircase is the only way downstairs. She'll have to come back up those stairs and through this room when she leaves. Let's hide where we can see and wait for her."

They split up and began searching for likely hiding places. The washroom was spacious, but crowded with washing machines, wringers, sinks, tubs, buckets of soap, and laundry baskets.

Bea attempted to slide into a space between two large tubs, but didn't fit. She looked inside several cupboards, but they were already stuffed full. She finally stopped in front of what appeared to be a very ordinary wall.

"It's perfect," she realized. On the wall several feet above the floor, were two silver knobs. Bea grabbed the knobs and pulled. A set of cupboard-like doors opened out from the wall, revealing the enclosed space of the service elevator.

She climbed in and settled on top of some canvas bags next to a bucket of Naptha powdered laundry soap. Fearing Miss Grim would return at any moment, Bea stuck her head back out and began anxiously looking for Walter. She finally spotted him standing at one of the sinks, gulping down a glass of water.

"Walter. Over here," Bea called to him in a whispery voice, as loud as she dared.

Walter whirled around. Catching sight of Bea, he lifted his hand and waved, but immediately turned back to the sink to refill his glass.

Bea opened her mouth, intending to urge Walter to hurry, but the words froze at the sound of footsteps ascending the stairs.

CHAPTER
9

Walter heard the soft clap of Miss Grim's footsteps ascending the stairs. He slapped frantically at the spigot, finally managing to turn off the flow of water. Still holding onto the water glass, he darted for the elevator. Water sloshed over the rim of the glass, dripping down his arm onto the floor.

Walter tipped the glass as he scrambled to climb in next to Bea, spilling what water remained into her lap. Bea swallowed her gasp of shock as the cold water instantly soaked through her pants. Somehow Walter managed to close the elevator doors, leaving a narrow opening to peer through.

Miss Grim stepped into view at the top of the staircase. She carried a large pile of rumpled clothing. The lower part of her face was hidden behind the clothes, but her cold, gray eyes peered over the worn soles on a pair of men's shoes weighing down the top of the pile.

She continued across the room towards the door and the adjacent service elevator that harbored the two spies.

Inside the elevator, Walter was twitching. His foot had a terrible itch. He longed to scratch it, but couldn't bring his hand within reach in the small crowded space.

Miss Grim was only a few feet away from the elevator doors when Walter shook his foot in an attempt to alleviate the itch. Somehow he managed to knock over the bucket of detergent. The edge of the bucket hit the elevator floor with a sharp metallic 'clang'. A puff of powdery soap crystals drifted up into Walter and Bea's faces.

At the sudden noise, Miss Grim let out a startled gasp and stopped in her tracks. She cocked her head, listening intently. Walter and Bea held their breath, paralyzed with fear, sure they were about to be caught.

Bea closed her eyes and imagined Miss Grim's cold gaze looking directly at her through the narrow opening in the elevator doors.

Walter and Bea expected, at any moment, the doors to the elevator would be jerked open and they would be discovered. Then came an unexpected and welcome interruption.

Someone else had entered the building and they could be heard enjoying a lively conversation as they neared the washroom.

"I can't remember when I've tasted a sweeter watermelon."

"I heard they trucked them here from Hermiston. They have the hot weather over there that brings on that sweet taste."

Bea recognized the voices of Vivian and Bell, two women who worked in the laundry. Bea sighed and slumped in relief.

"Well, hello Virginia," Bell said when the two women walked into the washroom and encountered Miss Grim.

"If you're bringing dirty laundry, just put it down anywhere."

"Oh there's my sweater," Vivian said.

From inside the closet Walter and Bea heard someone walk a short distance into the room and then return to the doorway.

"It's not laundry," Miss Grim answered Bell, bluntly. "I've been downstairs, gathering clothes for two men who just arrived this afternoon. I'm taking these over to the dormitory right now."

Bea's relief over their apparent escape from detection was short lived.

Earlier, when the bucket fell spilling the laundry detergent, a few of the tiny soap crystals had lodged in her nose. While the women talked she scrunched and rubbed and wiggled her nose, creating funny faces that made Walter want to laugh. But the tickling sensation only increased.

Beginning to panic, Bea pinched her nose closed with a thumb and forefinger and pressed her lips into a firm line in an effort to hold back a giant sneeze.

"If you'll excuse me I'd like to be on my way," Miss Grim said.

"We'll walk out with you," they heard Bell reply.

Bea sucked in a deep breath "Ah…, Ah…", Walter scrunched his shoulders, squinting his eyes in anticipation of the big blow.

Finally, all three women were heard moving away down the hall; and then, the faint sounds of the front door closing.

"A-tchoo!"

Tiny white bits sprayed from Bea's nose.

Walter pushed open the elevator doors and leaped out; he immediately ran from the room and down the hall.

Bea climbed out slowly; her energy and her fanciful notions about the glamorous life of a crime fighter seemed to have blown away with the sneeze. Her pants were stiff and scratchy where the spilled detergent had soaked into the damp material.

Wearily, she trailed after Walter and met up with him outside.

"I followed Miss Grim," he said, "and she didn't take the clothes into the dormitory like she said she was going to; she took them inside her apartment. She must be stealing them."

"We can't prove anything yet," Bea said.

"Maybe she'll try to sneak them into her car," Walter said.

"Yeah, maybe."

Bea's ruined pants chaffed her legs. She walked in an awkward, stiff-legged gait back to the apartment to change clothes.

Walter decided that spying really made a guy hungry and he ran back to the picnic area in hopes of finding just one more piece of cake.

It was late evening, darkness and quiet enveloped the Poor Farm. Lingering traces of the acrid, biting smoke from Walter's earlier barrage of firecrackers drifted into the attic room where Bea lay in bed, yawning and fighting sleep.

She wondered how her brother, Billy, and her father, had spent the holiday. She tried to picture the TB hospital on a hill east of Salem, and her mother standing at a window looking out at the fireworks set off in the city below.

Bea's last waking thoughts were prayers for her scattered family.

CHAPTER
10

O n the day following the Fourth of July celebration, the pleasant summer temperatures had plummeted and then continued unseasonably cool for the next three weeks. The skies above the farm hovered low in swirling patterns of gray.

Frequent rain showers kept Bea and Walter inside, playing board games and listening to the radio.

To their great disappointment, neither Walter nor Bea had uncovered anything suspicious regarding Miss Grim, in spite of a fair amount of covert listening and artful spying. Bea was itching to make a new entry into her book of Evidence and Clues.

Finally, this morning, the sun had risen with renewed intensity, leading a canopy of clear blue sky.

Bea sat on the broad stone rim of the water fountain with her legs immersed in the cool water and her toes brushing the pebbly bottom. She'd bunched her skirt in her lap, forming a pocket to hold the pink and white zinnias she'd gathered from the flowerbed bordering the driveway.

Selecting a white flower from the pile in her lap, she carefully slit the stem with her fingernail, then pulled the stem of a pink bloom through the opening. Soon a chain of blooms spilled across her lap.

Bea tipped her head, squinting in the bright sunlight, to admire Mrs. Paris, whose gray granite neck was already draped in bloom. Beside his mate, Mr. Paris, maintained his alert, benevolent watch.

"I didn't forget you," Bea told him. "See."

Leaning across Mrs. Paris, she draped the newly finished garland across his neck. The few leftover blooms she shook from her skirt into the fountain, where they bobbed and dipped under the gentle overhead spray.

Bea lifted her legs out of the water and slipped on her tennis shoes. The tips of her big toes poked out through holes worn in the canvas tops of her shoes. The laces had broken and been replaced with baling twine.

Bea headed for the clubhouse.

She suspected Walter was already there.

Remembering the mail she'd received yesterday, she made a quick detour back to the apartment to retrieve it.

A grain sack hung over the opening into the clubhouse.

On it Walter had written in black crayon.

W & B Detective Agency

Bea pushed aside the sack and ducked inside.

Walter sat cross-legged on the floor on his side of the clubhouse. With quick, downward jabs of his pocketknife he was whittling a sharp point at one end of a thin tree branch. His lap was covered with bits of wood and bark.

"Howdy," he said, in cowboy fashion.

"Howdy," Bea replied.

She plopped down on the quilt she'd spread over the flattened cardboard.

When she sat up, she had her nose pinched between her fingers. "What's that rotten smell?"

"I don't smell anything?"

"Don't you ever change your clothes after you work in the barn?" Bea suspected Walter's job of mucking out the milking stalls was the source of the bad odor.

"Not unless I have to," Walter answered, unconcerned. Walter blew at the tip of his finished arrow before dropping it into a fruit jar with half a dozen others he'd already finished.

"I got mail yesterday," Bea said, and held up the letter and the postcard she'd brought with her. She handed the postcard to Walter.

The picture on the front side was a cartoon drawing of a boy, barefoot and wearing overalls, standing in a peach orchard. From each hand hung a bucket, each bucket contained a single fuzzy, pink peach the size of a small watermelon. Printed across the bottom of the picture was the caption, Wenatchee — Best Fruit in the West.

Walter turned the card over and read the message.

Dear Bea,

   Finished picking cherries. Now working in a peach orchard. Doing good, only a few bee stings. A worker arrived yesterday, said he and another man hitched a ride on top of a railroad car. On the way here the train entered a tunnel, when it came out the other side the other man was gone. Guess he was blown off.

   Summer's almost over,

   See you soon,

                                                 Billy

"Wow, I wish I could do that," Walter mused, handing Bea the postcard.

85

"What, fall off a train?"

"No, stupid, ride a train. I wouldn't be dumb enough to fall off."

Bea let pass the opportunity to comment on just how dumb Walter might be.

She'd also received a letter from her mother and showed Walter the small painting on the back of the envelope.

"My mom's learning how to paint watercolor pictures from another patient at the hospital," she explained.

Walter admired the soft shades of a sunset brushed across the back of the envelope.

"She's really good. But what's this?" he asked. He pointed to a pencil drawing of a Plymouth Roadster in the upper right hand corner of the envelope. Its headlights had the appearance of eyes with dark centers and curled lashes, and the front grill turned up in a convincing smile.

A poem was printed next to the drawing.

Walter bent closer to read it.

If you want to purr like a kitten;
Come to Jack's Auto Park and get fixed by a Lamb.

"Huh?" Walter looked back at Bea under raised eyebrows.

"It's our last name, Lamb."

"Oh, yeah. Your dad's pretty funny."

Bea took back the envelope.

She retrieved the cigar box she kept in an apple crate, wedged into the vines. For a moment, she kept her back turned toward Walter, not wanting him to notice the tears that had welled up and threatened to spill down her face. She tenderly brushed her fingers over the envelope before she placed it in the cigar box.

She wished that all things were as quick to fix as a car.

Walter hopped to his feet. "I'm leaving." He closed his pocketknife against the side of his leg with a loud snap, and shoved it into his pocket. He brushed off his pants, flinging wood shavings in all directions.

"Keep your mess on your side," Bea complained, tossing back to his side the debris that had landed on her quilt.

"You should like it, wood smells really good."

"Maybe wood does, but there is something in here that smells really terrible."

Bea eyed the stuff piled on the shelves on Walter's side of the clubhouse. There didn't seem to be anything there that would give off such a bad odor. Then she noticed the rug he was sitting on; she bent closer and sniffed.

"Oh," she gasped, jerking away. "Walter, that thing you've been sitting on is what stinks."

"It's not a thing, it's an old worn-out horse blanket. Jiggs said I could keep it."

"The horse must have been worn-out too; it smells like he died while wearing it."

Walter bent down and put his nose close to the blanket. He sniffed slow and deep. "Ahh," he said, a look of pure pleasure spreading across his face like a smile. "Don't you just love the smell of damp horse blanket."

Bea grunted, shaking her head. At times like these it was hard to remember why Walter was such a good friend.

Outside in the brambly thicket of their clubhouse, Bea and Walter poked among the stickery canes searching for ripe blackberries to eat. The last few weeks of rain had spoiled much of the fruit, turning them soft and slushy or spotting them with puffs of white mold.

After a bit of searching they each had a handful to eat on their walk up to the house. Bea held her berries loosely cupped in her hand and tossed them one at a time into her mouth, savoring the sweet tartness. Walter tipped back his head and dumped the entire handful into his mouth.

Walter smacked his lips and a line of red juice dribbled off his chin.

Coming onto the laundry building, they heard the sounds of voices coming from inside the building through an open window. When they heard Miss Grim's name mentioned, they stopped in their tracks, like players in a game of "ice tag".

Instinctually, they ducked down and crept stealthily to the side of the building, where they crouched below the window.

Coming from directly above their heads, the voices were loud and clear.

"I confess Bell. I never did like that woman. She was in my class at Sandy High School: the graduating class of 1900. It was supposed to be a lucky year to graduate, beginning a new century and all. Can't say it's been too lucky though, what with a world war and now a economic depression."

"Yes that's true. But, why didn't you like her, Vivian?" Bell asked.

"Can't say I really knew her. But she always looked like she'd just swallowed a lemon. As far as I ever noticed, she didn't have any friends. She walked home from school with her two younger brothers. And I heard those two were as ornery as they come."

"It's a shame," Bell muttered.

"Yeah, even I felt sorry for her after the tragedy."

"What tragedy? What happened?"

"Just a few weeks before high school graduation her family's house burned to the ground in the middle of the night. Her and her two brothers escaped, but her mom and stepfather died in the fire."

Died? Bea felt a lump forming in her throat and her chest seemed too tight as if it would stop her breath. She bit her lip, confused that her comfortable feelings of dislike for Miss Grim could be stirred up by feelings of sympathy. And the scars she'd noticed on Miss Grim's hand. Were they the result of burns she'd suffered in the fire?

Bea resumed listening. "At the time," Vivian was explaining to Bell, "the gossip going around town held that the stepfather was downright mean, and a drunk. Most people thought he was probably the cause of the fire somehow. I never heard what happened to Virginia or her brothers after the fire. She never showed up for graduation."

With these words, the conversation ended, followed by a squeaking sound that Bea recognized as coming from laundry carts being wheeled across the linoleum floor. When there were no more sounds at the window, Walter and Bea moved away from the building.

"Now you know why Miss Grim is so mean," Walter said with his usual bravado. She's just like her stepfather."

Bea didn't comment right away. When she did, her voice was quiet and thoughtful, as if speaking to herself.

"Maybe she's mean because of him."

When they got back to the house, they sat on the porch steps.

"What I'm trying to figure out," Walter said, "Is how this new information about Miss Grim will help us to prove she's the thief. A really good detective leaves no clue unturned.

"I figure that a fire like the one that killed Miss Grim's parents would be big news in a small town. It must have been written about in the newspaper."

"Probably," Bea said. "But how would we get a newspaper from 1900? That's thirty five years ago."

"From the Library. Last year I went to the library to do a school report on the Great War, they have a room full of newspapers from way, way back."

"I guess we could look. But I don't know how a fire that happened thirty-five years go will be of any help."

"Come on, let's find my mom. If you ask her to take us to the library she's sure to say yes.

The next afternoon Walter and Bea climbed from the back seat of the Briggs' Plymouth and walked up the steps to the Eastside Branch of the county library. The building was handsome, made entirely of red bricks. Several of the tall arched windows on two sides of the building were topped with stained glass.

The front doors opened onto a shallow foyer with a tiled granite floor. Mounted above a second set of doors a bronze plaque warned "Quiet Please".

Bea put her finger against her lips then looked at Walter and made a 'Shhh' sound before she pushed the doors open.

Inside the library Walter approached the librarian seated at the checkout desk. The name, Miss Blake, was printed on a name tag pinned to her blouse.

"We would like to look at newspapers," Walter said, straining to maintain a properly hushed voice.

Before she responded, Miss Blake removed her glasses from the bridge of her nose leaving them dangling against her chest from a chain around her neck.

"Current or past?" she asked.

"Past," Bea answered, "very past."

"Follow me," the librarian whispered, rising from her chair.

She led them to a small ell at the back of the main reading room.

"Which newspapers are you seeking?"

"We are seeking," Walter explained, trying to match the librarian's formal manner, "all the editions of the *Sandy Sentinel* newspaper published in the year 1900."

Miss Blake returned her glasses to her nose and moved efficiently along a wall of shelves, studying the labels on the spines of stiff cardboard binders. The chain attached to the arms of her glasses swung gently along the sides of her face. They reminded Bea of the loose flapping jowls of a St. Bernard dog.

"Here we are."

The librarian straightened and slid one of the binders from the shelf and carried it to a table in the center of the room.

"The *Sandy Sentinel* only puts out two editions a week, so the whole year of 1900 is contained inside this one cover. Please be careful. The pages are fragile."

"I appreciate fragile," Walter responded.

Bea had to quickly bite her lip to keep back a bark of laughter.

"See that you do," the librarian said soberly, before leaving them to return to her desk.

"Where do we start?" Walter asked.

"Vivian told Bell the fire happened before she graduated," Bea reminded Walter. "So, if we start with the June paper and search back towards January, we won't miss it."

Walter agreed.

They opened the binder and turned the pages until they located the June 5, 1900 edition of the *Sandy Sentinel*. A photograph of the twenty-five students in the Sandy High School graduating class took up most of the front page.

Bea scanned the names printed below the picture. A Miss Virginia Grim was not listed. But they did locate the laundry worker, Vivian, a tall girl in the back row. She wore a lacy dress with puff sleeves and a high neck that brushed the bottom of her chin. Roses were stuck into the knot of hair on top of her head.

With Walter scanning the columns to the left of the centerfold and Bea covering the right side, it didn't take long before they had looked over every page of newsprint back to the May seventh edition.

Walter yelled, "Here it is."

"Shh...," Bea warned.

Walter clamped his hand over his mouth and pointed at a headline on page two.

HOUSE FIRE TRAGEDY

At 2:00 a.m. on the morning of May 5th, The Sandy Volunteer Fire Department responded to a fire at the Spangle residence on Bluff road. Regretfully the home was fully ablaze and proceeded to burn to the ground before help arrived.

Don Spangle and his wife Dora were unable to escape and died inside. Mr. Spangle's three stepchildren, Virginia, Vern and Buck, jumped from a second story window and survived with only minor burns.

All of the family's possessions were lost. It is not known at this time what will happen to the three children. There are no known relatives.

Bea turned ahead several editions, but there were no more mentions of the fire.

When they were once again outside, they waited on the library steps for Mrs. Briggs to pick them up.

"That must have been terrible to lose both her parents and

everything they owned," Bea told Walter.

"Maybe not if her stepfather was as mean as Vivian said."

"She must have missed her mother though," Bea said.

For a while, there seemed nothing more to say, so they rested their elbows on their knees and watched the traffic and the people passing on the sidewalk.

Walter was first to return to the subject of the fire.

"The newspaper article said Miss Grim's brother's names were Vern and Buck. I'm sure I've heard those names mentioned recently. I just can't remember where."

"I still don't know how a fire that happened thirty five years ago is going to help us prove Miss Grim is a thief?" said Bea.

"Unless," Walter said, "after the fire she and her brothers had to steal to eat. The article did say the family lost all their possessions. Maybe once she began stealing she just couldn't stop herself."

"Maybe," Bea agreed, although not sounding convinced.

"Mom's here," Walter said, watching the familiar Plymouth turn the corner and pull up to the curb. As they climbed into the back seat of the automobile Walter was still trying to remember where he'd heard about two brothers named Vern and Buck.

CHAPTER
11

The sow's sharp-toed hoofs scratched at the ground in her enclosure, sending a spray of dry, fine dust across her back. With her flat, speckled snout she nudged the toes of Bea's tennis shoes, leaving behind a string of drool and bits of grain. Giving up on Bea's shoes as a source of food, the sow lowered her head and turned away to join the rest of the herd napping in an area of wet dirt below a leaky water spigot.

Bea was alone and bored. Right after lunch Walter had gone into Portland with his mother, and wouldn't be returning until late afternoon.

After eating lunch, Bea had wondered about the yard rather aimlessly and finally perched on the top rail of the fence surrounding the pigsty. Bea rested her elbows on her knees while she watched the equally lethargic pig saunter away across the barren pen and drop her bulk into a space between two snoring companions. After a bit of twitching and shifting the sow settled into the cool mud. Apparently satisfied, she flopped onto one side and closed her eyes.

Up on the fence, Bea closed her eyes and tried to imagine herself settling into the cool depths of a winter snow bank.

But the stubborn afternoon sun was burning a hot patch across her shoulders, denying her this imagined pleasure.

Bea sighed and stretched out her arms before swinging her legs over the rail to the outside of the enclosure and jumping down. Lacking a snowbank, she'd decided to pay a visit to the ice storage shed.

Clyde, who supervised the loading dock, often invited Walter and Bea inside the shed where crates of vegetables were stored among blocks of ice stacked in sawdust. Using an ice pick, Clyde would knock off a fist-sized hunk of ice for each of them, and then drop it into a rolled tube of newspaper to be carried and licked like an ice cream cone.

Today though, when Bea arrived at the shed, there was no sign of Clyde. The large doors, hanging from tracks high above Bea's head, were rolled shut. Disappointed, Bea sat down on the edge of the dock and dangled her legs, tapping her heels against the wood and feeling very sorry for herself.

She considered spying on Miss Grim, feeling a tickle of pleasure at the possibility of catching her in an act of thievery when Walter wasn't around to take the credit. But she knew Miss Grim had worked the night shift and was now inside her apartment sleeping. It didn't seem very likely that she'd discover anything new today.

Bea jumped from the dock. Might as well visit Lila at her office.

When she arrived at the office door, Lila was seated at her desk, bent over a ledger of purchase orders. She briefly glanced at Bea and mumbled something around the pencil she held between her teeth.

Bea slid into the empty chair beside Lila's desk. In short order the continual clackity-clack from the adding machine and the insect-like whirring of the ceiling fan gave Bea a headache. She shifted her legs on the metal chair seat. Sweat was pooling beneath her knees.

"There's some lemonade in the ice box at home," Lila said, remembering to remove the pencil while she talked, yet maintaining her attention to the ledgers. "Why don't you go and pour yourself a big glass. Try to stay cool."

Bea answered with a slow, deep sigh.

She slid off the chair, leaving damp smudges on the metal seat.

Outside again, she took the route through the oak grove behind the dormitory. She stepped into the shade under a large oak tree where a thermometer had been nailed to the trunk. By standing on her tiptoes, she was able to see the mark at the top of the rising, red bubble. It read 99 degrees, Fahrenheit. She dropped to her heels and continued toward home, feeling more and more miserable.

Inside the house, the window shades had been lowered to keep out the heat. Bea squinted in the gloom and stumbled up the stairs. The air inside the apartment was still and oppressive, but at least she was out of the sun.

Bea took the pitcher from the refrigerator and poured herself a tall glass of lemonade. After returning the pitcher, she walked into the sitting room and set the glass on the trunk in front of the sofa. Before sitting down she crossed the room to the radio.

The wood knob turned on with a soft click and the radio immediately began to hum and crackle, a yellow light backlit the numbers on the dial. Bea twisted the knob to change the station. She flipped past the drama that Mrs. Briggs listened to in her kitchen while she ironed. She paused briefly to catch the sounds of several orchestras. They all seemed to be playing music equally as slow and dreary as the day.

Finding nothing of interest she turned off the radio and lay down on the sofa to sip her lemonade and look through the newest edition of *Silver Screen* magazine.

Bea didn't remember falling asleep, but she found herself waking up with the magazine still open on her lap and the glass emptied and resting on the trunk.

Bea sat up and rubbed her face. Her cheek felt prickly and poked where it had rested against a crocheted afghan while she slept.

The clock in the kitchen showed, 4:30 p.m.

Maybe Walter's back from town, she thought.

After putting the dirty glass in the sink, she left the apartment to find out.

Outside the Briggs' apartment, Bea stood with her ear pressed against the door. Even with the extra effort to hold perfectly still and close her eyes, she couldn't detect any noises or movement coming from inside. Realizing she could check to see if their car had returned, she headed outside.

Coming around to the front of the garage she found the doors still open and the space empty. For some reason, the absence of the Briggs' car released the flood of anger and resentment that had been stirring inside Bea all day.

With her hands clinched, she took a step inside the garage and yelled, "It's not fair."

"It's not fair," she said a second time, her voice now a mere whisper. "I want to go home."

Bea turned her back to the garage and walked away. It's just not fair, she continued to brood as she headed for the oak grove to recheck the thermometer. Billy gets to travel wherever he wants. Daddy's letters make it sound like he enjoys working on cars, and doesn't even miss the grocery store. And Mom has a new friend, a lot nicer than Walter. Mom's probably forgotten about me, she's so busy painting.

The almost certain untruth of this final thought brought with it a stab of guilt, but Bea pushed it aside. She was bored and miserably hot. No one seemed to care.

Last night Bea had brought her box of letters into bed and reread them all before going to sleep. A line in one of her mother's letters had stayed in her mind long after she'd put them away.

"…I know you will find that God has something wonderful planned for you this summer."

Well, Bea decided, if this was God's idea of a wonderful summer, then God sure didn't know much about pleasing young girls. Or maybe, Bea wondered, with a trace of anxiety, there was something she needed to do to get God's attention.

Stepping into the shade beneath the oak tree, Bea could see the red column inside the thermometer had risen to 102 degrees.

Bea sat down at the base of the tree in a grassy dip between the protruding knots on two knarled roots. The tree trunk's rough bark poked through her thin shirt into her back.

Bea closed her eyes. She began to imagine the heat inside her body rising up and out the top of her head, continuing up the trunk of the tree until it reached the thermometer, where the red liquid in the bubble began to boil.

"Hey, Bea. I'm back."

At the sound of Walter's voice, the glass bubble burst, sending out a spray of red liquid. Bea's eyes snapped open.

Walter ran across the grass toward her. He was wearing his 'go to town clothes' except for the shoes, which didn't surprise Bea. Mrs. Briggs was always threatening to nail them to his feet, just like you'd do to a horse. Bea imagined he'd pulled off his socks and shoes while still in the car on the way home from town.

Even though she'd been longing for his company all afternoon, when he finally appeared, full of energy and good cheer, she couldn't even bring herself to say hello.

Walter didn't seem to notice.

"Boy, I had a great day," he boasted. "We ate lunch in a restaurant at the very top of a real skyscraper. I had a chocolate milkshake. It came in a tall silver glass, as big as a pitcher. I filled up my drinking glass three times. Then we met my dad, but he wasn't ready to leave, so mom took me to the movie."

Bea knew she should say something nice to Walter about his fun day, but the more he talked the crankier she felt.

"Soooo." Bea finally answered. "When my mom gets home she'll take me to get a milkshake whenever I want."

Walter was so filled with himself and his day that he took little notice of Bea's sarcastic reply.

"Don't you want to know what movie I saw?"

"Not really."

"Well, I'll tell you anyway, *Tarzan the Ape Man*. I could ask mom to take me another time and you can go with us."

"Yeah, maybe."

"Do you want to come with me to the dairy barn to find Jiggs? I want to tell him about the movie."

Bea shrugged her shoulders, but stood up.

"Yeah, okay."

She brushed away the loose grass clippings clinging to the seat of her shorts before falling into step beside Walter.

They left the neatly mowed lawns of the housing complex and followed a shortcut to the dairy through a wild, unkempt field. The shaggy, dry grass tickled their bare legs. Grasshoppers, startled by their steps, leaped out of the grass like shooting stars beneath their feet.

Bea trailed behind Walter. The sun burned so hot on the top of her head, Bea was sure she could hear her hair crackle. She stuck out her lower lip and blew a gentle puff of air upward, momentarily lifting her damp bangs off her forehead.

They walked steadily without talking for several minutes, buoyed along by the swishing sounds of the parting grass. Walter finally noticed Bea was keeping unusually quiet. When he turned to show her a grasshopper he'd captured in his hands her face wore a scowl.

"What's wrong with you?" Walter asked.

"Nothing, I'm just hot."

Bea wiped away a trickle of sweat trailing down the back of her neck.

Walter opened his hands and tossed the grasshopper up into the air. He watched until it dropped out of sight in the grass.

They kept on across the field until Bea stopped suddenly and gave her right foot an angry shake. She was trying to dislodge a grasshopper that seemed content to remain firmly attached to her shoestring.

"Afraid of a little bug?" Walter snickered.

"No, but I don't have to take it with me."

Bea's scowl deepened as they resumed walking.

"If you weren't such a city girl, a few bugs and a little heat wouldn't make you so crabby. Hot weather doesn't bother me because I'm from the country and I'm tough, like Tarzan."

"I'm just as tough as you."

"No, you're not."

"Yes, I am.

"Well, prove it then."

Walter and Bea had arrived at a gate in the barbed wire fence surrounding the pasture, north of the dairy barn. Walter lifted the rope loop securing the gate to the fence post. They both leaped on the gate to catch a ride as it swung open over a dirt road.

The road, bounded on both sides by barbed wire fencing, cut across the north pasture all the way to the barn. Bea was first to jump from the gate and land on the road.

"If you're so tough," Walter said, returning to their earlier conversation, "take off your shoes and go barefoot like me."

"If I wanted to, I could go barefoot. I just don't feel like it.

"Sounds like a 'Sissy' excuse to me.

Walter gathered himself on the top bar of the gate, swaying a little before launching into a rather Tarzan inspired leap. He landed with a soft thud.

Showoff, Bea thought, but didn't bother to say so out loud.

Walter closed the gate and replaced the loop over the post.

The road followed the upward incline of the pasture for several hundred yards before it disappeared from sight over the crest of a hill. On the other side of the hill the pasture dropped steeply away toward the barn. After the recent days of dry, hot weather, the wheels of passing farm vehicles had churned the road's packed dirt surface into a thick layer of fine dust.

Walter pointed up the road in the direction of the barn.

"I bet you can't run all the way without your shoes."

Bea peered up the road, shading her eyes with one hand, squinting in the bright light. In the distance, the air hovering above the road was fuzzy with heat.

Bea hesitated. She knew Walter's feet were callused from going barefoot so often.

Maybe it was only a foolish impulse, one she'd regret, but Bea found herself taken up with the notion that all the injustice's of this miserably hot day would be wiped away in the tracks of her flying bare feet. She knew what she needed to do, not to prove anything to Walter, but for herself.

Bea bent down and began to untie her shoes.

She left them hanging over the gate, tied together by their laces. Without saying a word to Walter, she faced down the road and began to run. Walter, with a rather smug look on his face, leaned back against the gate and watched.

At first, the soft layer of fine, powdery dirt felt as warm and soothing as a walk across a feather bed. With each step, dirt puffed up between her toes and settled around her ankles. Running stirred the air and lifted the hair that hung limply over her damp neck and forehead.

Bea had covered nearly half the distance to the spot where the road crested the hill before she noticed the first twinges of discomfort. When she'd started out, she'd felt only a soothing, gentle heat on the soles of her feet. Now they were becoming painfully tender and uncomfortably hot.

Bea's steps slowed. She glanced back over her shoulder. Walter was still waiting at the gate. Looking past the gate, Bea spotted Mr. Briggs approaching across the field.

Walter cupped his hands to his mouth and shouted, "You'll never make it."

Bea faced ahead, pressed her lips into a determined line, and pushed on.

Her breaths were coming in shallow gasps when she reached the top of the incline and started down the backside of the hill. The sight of the barn brought momentary relief. Yet, when she realized the great distance that remained before she'd reach the shady area underneath the barn eaves, a faint moan escaped Bea's lips.

She'd never make it.

It had become impossible to ignore the pain radiating across the bottoms of her feet. The dusty road had become a path of burning coals.

Her eyes darted back and forth across the road, frantically searching for a way to escape the blistering heat. Lush green pasture bordered both sides of the road, but Bea was cut off, imprisoned between barbed wire fences. The grass on her side of the fence was yellow, dry and sparse. The only green plants were thistles, easy to spot with their bushy, purple, flower heads.

There was no place to go.

CHAPTER
12

Bea was frantic. Her steps wavered, then slowed, and finally stopped. She stood stork-like, lifting first one foot and then the other, while twisting her head to search for a spot to get relief.

Tears blurred her vision. She almost missed seeing the apple crate lying bottom side up against a fence post; its frame of pale, bleached wood, camouflaged in the dry grass. Bea heedlessly brushed past a patch of thistles in her rush for the safety of the crate.

She dropped down on top of the hard wood slats, shifting her body until she was finally able to lift her feet off the ground. There she sat; legs crossed, the soles of her feet turned up.

Deep sighs of relief escaped Bea's lips. With the back of her hand, she wiped away the beads of sweat dotting her upper lip. After she'd had a moment to savor her escape, Bea bent over to check the condition of her feet. They were coated in dust. She tried to brush it off, but the attempt proved so painful she soon stopped. The bottoms of her toes were hot and tender, and even under a layer of dust, looked red. On both feet patches of skin were already puffy from rising blisters.

Bea's throat felt so parched it was difficult to swallow. She sat up and looked around. There wasn't another person in sight. She was alone, marooned. A grasshopper landed in her lap, but quickly jumped away.

"I can't expect much help from you," she thought.

Then she remembered Walter. Where was he? Why hadn't he followed her?

For a while, she gazed hopefully back along the road in the direction she'd come, expecting at any moment to see the top of Walter's head pop into view as he approached the top of the hill. While she waited, she pictured how he'd look: running full tilt; his legs churning; one arm raised; her tennis shoes swinging by their laces in circles above his head.

Bea waited. The heat hovered above the road in shimmering rows. The top of her head felt slick with heat.

Walter still didn't come.

Finally, Bea turned her attention to the empty barnyard. She knew Jiggs and the other workers were inside the barn preparing for the evening milking. She thought about yelling, to attract attention, but her throat was dry and tight, and she was simply too tired and heavy with heat to make the effort.

Gazing past the peeked barn roof to the farthest pasture, Bea could see the cows, no longer grazing, but heading toward the barn at a leisurely pace. One tan colored cow pulled in front of the others, and gradually the rest of the herd fell into single file behind her. They followed a well-worn path; a path that at this distance appeared as a thin brown crease in the grassy field.

While occupied watching the cows, Bea almost forgot about her injured feet and her increasing anger at Walter. She even smiled at the idea of cows behaving like school children, lining up to go inside from recess; Jiggs, their teacher, waiting at the door, ringing the bell. Bea watched until the last cow disappeared from sight behind the barn.

The sun was now low in the west and shone directly into Bea's face. She wondered how long she'd been sitting here. Gnawing hunger pains served up vivid reminders of the supper she was missing. She licked her dry lips and envied the cows; by now they were munching grain in their sheltered stalls.

Increasing pain in Bea's neck and back were beginning to compete with the pain in her feet. Twisting and stretching brought little relief. Restless, and needing to change positions, Bea scooted to the edge of the crate nearest the fence post, intending to lean against it.

The instant her back touched the post she yelped in surprise and jerked away, realizing too late that she'd touch the post at the point where the barbed wire was attached.

With this final indignity, Bea's last bit of courage dissolved. She dropped her head and covered her face with her hands. Tears flowed unchecked down her cheeks and dripped from her chin.

At this dark moment a movement along the top of the hill caught her attention. She shaded her eyes with her hand and stared intently up the road. Someone was coming. Bea blinked rapidly to clear her blurry vision. Whoever that someone was, they were advancing at a steady pace down the road in her direction.

Was Walter finally coming?

"Oh, no!" Bea gasped, grabbing the sides of the crate in surprise.

Her rescuer, rapidly looming ever larger, wasn't Walter, or Jiggs, or anyone Bea could have ever expected.

Moving along in her usual brisk and deliberate manner,

Miss Grim was almost on top of Bea before she saw her.

Miss Grim stumbled to a halt. She sucked in a startled, "Oh," and then quickly gathered herself.

"What are you doing sneaking around and scaring a person?" she scolded.

"Miss Grim, I, I…." Bea took a calming breath and tried a second time to speak. She pointed to her feet while mumbling something about missing shoes, and Tarzan, and life not being fair, and Walter's callused feet.

From Miss Grim's confused expression, it was clear she understood little of Bea's explanation, but enough to prompt her to step over the dry grass, avoiding the thistles, to look more closely at Bea's feet.

That one look was enough to uncover the reason for Bea's tears and unusual behavior.

Later, Bea was to doubt what happened next. In that unguarded moment when Miss Grim leaned toward her, Bea, who was too worn out to shy away, looked directly into Miss Grim's face. There, in the steel gray eyes, she saw a flicker of pity. Even the deep lines on Miss Grim's forehead and around her mouth, evidence of her usual pinched expression, smoothed and softened. Her hand reached out as if to cradle an injured foot.

But then, just as suddenly, Miss Grim straightened and stepped back onto the road, her face a picture of disapproval.

"You've certainly gotten yourself into a pickle," she said. "I suppose I'll have to find someone to come and fetch you."

"Thank you," Bea sniffed.

When Miss Grim backed onto the road, Bea noticed the battered black handles on a pair of wire cutters sticking out of her white uniform pocket. Bea recognized the battered handles. She'd often seen Jiggs using those same cutters to repair barbed wire fences.

Miss Grim caught the direction of her glance.

"I saw these fall off the back of Jiggs truck," she explained curtly. "I was on my way to return them."

With these parting words she strode away.

A few minutes after Miss Grim disappeared inside the barn, Jiggs was coming up the road in his truck. He pulled to a stop across from Bea. Bea shielded her eyes from the cloud of dust that billowed up from beneath the truck's wheels and slowly settled again.

"My, my, what have we here?" Jiggs said, as he climbed out of the truck. He easily lifted Bea off the crate and into the front seat of the cab.

"Heat got to ya?" Jiggs asked.

Bea nodded her head, too exhausted to answer questions.

"All right now," Jiggs said. He shifted gears and worked the foot pedals. The truck jerked forward several times and then ran smoothly up the road.

Back at the house he carried Bea up the stairs to the apartment she shared with Lila.

Lila soon had her settled on the sofa with her feet soaking in a pan of cool water. After Bea gratefully gulped down a tall glass of water she sank back into the sofa's plump cushions and closed her tired eyes. Lila gently wiped her dusty face with a cool, damp washcloth, erasing the tracks left by her tears.

For a while, Bea slept, then awoke when Lila dropped a chunk of ice into the pan of water. Seeing that Bea was awake, Lila sat down beside her.

"Feeling Better?"

"Yes, thanks Lila."

"You're welcome, Honey."

Lila lay her arm around Bea's shoulders and squeezed her close to her side.

"Are you ready to tell me what happened?"

Bea looked down at her feet, wriggling her toes to stir the water. She sucked on her lower lip and pondered her answer. It all seemed so foolish now.

"I, I was just so hot." Bea began. "Life just didn't seem fair. Walter was having a good time with his mom downtown, and then I kept thinking about my mom and dad and Billy and how everyone seemed to be getting along just fine without me this summer. Then Walter came home and … " Bea continued with her story while Lila listened and nodded, occasionally smiling.

"…When Walter dared me to run down the road barefoot, I just did it. I was so tied in knots about everything that I thought I had to do something or I'd burst. So I ran."

"I see," Lila said, patting Bea's hand before getting up to go into the kitchen. She returned with a towel over her shoulder and carrying a glass of milk and a cheese sandwich on a plate.

The sight of food brought Bea's attention back to her empty stomach.

"You slept through dinner." Lila set the meal on the trunk in front of the sofa.

"If I let you soak those feet much longer your toes just might grow fins."

Bea giggled and for the first time that day felt a spirit of hope nudge away at her despair.

"Now lift your feet out of the water and wrap them in this towel."

With careful, cautious pats, Bea dried her ankles and feet. After they were wrapped in the towel and resting on a sofa pillow, she reached eagerly for her sandwich.

Lila carried away the pan of water before settling herself into the rocking chair on the other side of the trunk facing the sofa.

"In the days when I was a girl," Lila began, her voice mellow and steady, like the sway of the rocker, "a few years older than you are now, I was confronted with a disappointment so immense I thought I couldn't live through it. I ran too. Not down a hot, dusty road, but I ran just the same.

"You could say this trunk played a big part in the events that led up to my flight." Lila paused in her rocking to lean forward and draw her fingertips lightly over the trunk's smooth varnished top.

"What happened?" Bea urged, feeling refreshed from the food and eager to hear Lila's story.

CHAPTER
13

Lila folded her hands in her lap and continued with her story.

"In the days of my childhood, girls were expected to learn the skills necessary to become competent seamstresses. Even before I'd reached an age to start school, my mother sat me down in our parlor in the afternoons and taught me to sew a straight seam. When my finished seams passed inspection, I was taught to darn over holes in socks and mend the tears in my clothes."

At this remembrance Lila chuckled and paused in her story.

"You might not guess, looking at me now, but back then I was skinny as a pencil and quite a tomboy. I'd rush outside to play in the fields and barns whenever I got the chance. I'm sure my mother thought I'd curb my rowdy ways if I had the responsibility of mending my torn dresses myself."

Bea smiled at the image of a young, and not very repentant, Lila, sitting on a stool in the parlor and with small, neat stitches, reattaching the sleeve of her dress.

"Well, anyway," Lila continued. When I was ten years old I was given a sampler to complete of more difficult decorative stitches. That was also the year I received this trunk as a birthday gift.

"Along with the trunk came a responsibility. My mother assured me that by the time I graduated from high school my trunk would be filled with things I had sewn."

"What kinds of things?" Bea asked, before tossing the last bit of sandwich into her mouth.

"Oh, pillowcases, table cloths, bed covers, lace doilies, dish cloths, all things I would need in my own home when I became a bride.

"Most of my girlfriends thought this quite a tedious chore, but not me. For something else happened the year I received this trunk; a family moved in next door and they had a son named William.

"William was older than I was by three years, but from the moment I saw him peering over the fence that separated our front yards, I had fallen in love and I knew someday we'd be married. I never told anyone about this belief, not my girl-friends, not my parents, not even William.

"As soon as I'd finish one sewing project I'd begin another, all the while dreaming about my future life with William. Just to show you how stubborn and certain I really was, I secretly monogrammed a set of pillowcases with the initials LM and WM.

"The years passed and the trunk began to fill. After William graduated from high school he continued living next door and went to work at his father's harness shop. For the next three years we were both occupied with our own activities and our paths seldom crossed. Finally, I too walked down the aisle to receive my diploma.

"That evening, after returning home from the graduation ceremony, I took the tassel from my cap and tied it to the clasp on my trunk. The time of my change from a girl to a woman had arrived. All my hopes and dreams were stitched into those starched and folded linens so carefully stacked inside my trunk.

"All that summer I waited for William to reveal his true feelings toward me. I blush now to think how shamelessly I lingered on the front porch those warm summer evenings in anticipation of the long-awaited moment when he would leap the fence and declare his love."

"However, my life was to take a different turn than I'd anticipated. One very ordinary August morning, I was in the kitchen spreading marmalade on toast, when my mother returned from visiting next door with the news that William was engaged. The girl's name was Faye. They were to be married on Thanksgiving Day.

"I was spared the pain of attending their wedding when my family left town for the holiday. But I really only postponed our meeting because they were returning to live next door in Williams' family home.

When they returned from their honeymoon, I watched from the front window as William and his new bride climbed from the carriage and unloaded their bags. They were in such high spirits, smiling and talking gaily as they lugged their bags up the porch stairs and disappeared inside William's house."

"Oh Lila," Bea responded tenderly, "that must have been awful."

"If there was ever a brokenhearted girl, it was me that day. I suppose I had the notion if I wanted something bad enough I could make it happen."

At this point Lila paused in her story telling.

"Let me refill your water glass and get a drink myself," she said. "All this talking is giving me a dry throat."

While Lila was in the kitchen her words settled around Bea's heart, stirring up a memory of her own.

It was almost unheard of for her father to miss a day of work at the grocery store. But on that morning, nearly two years ago, he had missed work to accompany her mother to a consultation with Dr. Shire about the seriousness of Elizabeth's persistent cough and lack of energy. Bea had begged to be allowed to stay home from school until they returned from the doctors. Her father hadn't argued.

She'd waved to her parents until their delivery van turned the corner at the end of the street before fleeing to her bedroom and falling across the bed.

"Mother can't have tuberculosis.

I need her.

I won't let her be sick."

In spite of her wishes, or prayers, when her parents returned they brought heartbreaking news. Her mother left the next day for an extended stay at the sanatorium in Salem.

Lila returned with the water and eased back into the rocker. Bea shifted her position on the sofa, carefully resetting her feet, anxious to hear the rest of Lila's story.

"...I had never felt so lonely and confused. Honey, I ran from my loneliness just like you ran from yours today. Not down a country road, but all the way to San Francisco."

"Did you really run all that way?"

"Not on two legs, but it was running just the same. I packed my bags and left the very next morning by train, to stay at my cousin's home."

"What happened in San Francisco?" Bea asked anxiously while lifting the edge of the blanket to her face to hide a yawn.

"Well, I sulked and moped for several weeks, proving to be a very unpleasant guest I'm sure. Then, one afternoon I was alone in the house, sitting in the window seat that over-looked San Francisco Bay. My aunt and cousin had left to pay a call on a neighbor. The frequent morning fog was especially thick that day and had lingered late so that the water in the bay remained shrouded in mist.

"I could see nothing of the blue sea I knew was out there, lapping at the edges of the boardwalks and fish stalls. There was no sign of the floating piers crowded with gently bobbing boats of all colors and sorts.

"It was that experience that helped me realize I had lost sight of all of life's wonderful possibilities by focusing on the fog of my disappointment and despair. I slid from the window seat and scampered upstairs to my bedroom. With a new vision and sense of purpose, I quickly changed into my 'afternoon calling clothes'. I prettied my face and hair before racing out of the house toward the train station to purchase my ticket home.

"Soon after my return, my mother died and I became the sole woman and caretaker of the house and my father. A year after William and Faye wed, they had their first and only child, a girl they named Elizabeth."

At this point in Lila's story, Bea instinctively leaned toward Lila and a look of astonishment spread across her face.

"Was it my Elizabeth? Bea gasped. "I mean my mother?" she giggled nervously.

"That's right. Your Grandpa and Grandpa Moore are the very same William and Faye. I practically raised your mother. She spent as much time at my house as she did at home.

"Your mother was a teenager when my father died. I sold our house, and with the experience I'd gained helping raise your mother, I was able to secure a job as a nanny with a family in San Francisco. The father of the family owned an import shipping company and over the next twenty years I made numerous trips with the family to the Orient."

"Tell me about the Orient?" Bea begged.

Lila raised her hands from her lap and placed them on

the arms of the rocker. "I think that's enough for one night. I know a girl who should be getting some sleep right now instead of staying awake listening to an old woman prattle on." Rather nimbly she scooted her plump frame to the edge of the chair and stood.

Bea lay back on the sofa, her head sinking into the pillow while her mouth opened wide in a deep, satisfying yawn.

"I think you'd better sleep on the sofa tonight," Lila said. "I'd probably send us both to the hospital if I tried to carry you up those stairs to your bed. I'll go fetch your things."

Lila returned with Bea's nightgown along with some ointment and thick socks.

She helped Bea undress and slip her nightgown over her head and around her legs. Bea stretched out on the sofa and closed her eyes, exhausted from her eventful day. Lila smoothed a cool, moist cream over the bottoms of her feet before wrapping them with strips of cotton cloth and slipping on a pair of socks.

"Good night, Lila."

"Good night, Bea. Sleep well."

Lila kissed Bea gently on the forehead before turning off the lamp, leaving the room in semi-darkness. The pale orange glow of the setting sun filtered into the room through the west-facing windows.

Bea was drifting into sleep when she heard a knock at the front door, followed by the scrape of the kitchen chair and the tapping sound of Lila's shoes crossing the room.

The door rattled and opened.

"How's Bea doing?"

Bea recognized Walter's voice.

"I'm sorry about her feet. I didn't know. You see my father called me to come home and change out of my good clothes and then my mother told me to…"

"That's quite all right, Walter," Lila interrupted. "I'm sure she'll understand."

"Can I see her? I've some very important news that I need to tell her."

"Bea's already asleep. Whatever it is, I'm sure it can wait until tomorrow."

"Oh, alright. Bye."

"Goodnight, Walter."

Lila's steps retreated to the back of the apartment and her bedroom door closed.

Walter's appearance at the door reminded Bea that she needed to talk to him as soon as possible. She had remembered, with increasing suspicion, the wire cutters she'd spotted in Miss Grim's pocket that afternoon. And then there was Miss Grim's hasty and awkward explanation that she was returning the cutters to Jiggs.

Why would Miss Grim do Jiggs a favor?

Something else about Miss Grim's appearance was nagging at Bea. Bea recalled how Miss Grim looked as she walked away from Bea toward the barn. Her shoes and the bottom edge of her white uniform had been spotted with dust and one of her shoelaces had come untied. Bea remembered watching it bouncing in the dust beside her foot as she walked.

Why would Miss Grim, who always wore uniforms that were squeaky-clean, starched and polished, ever step foot on that dusty road? Something more sinister than returning a pair of lost wire cutters had to be behind Miss Grim's trip to the barn. Bea was sure of it.

Maybe she'd been planning to sell those too. But why would she be taking them back to the barn? Bea could hardly wait to talk to Walter. He could question Jiggs and see if he'd really lost those wire cutters.

CHAPTER
14

Two days had passed since her ordeal on the road. Bea was restless and "bustin' at the seams" to tell Walter about finding Miss Grim with the wire cutters. Even an amateur sleuth, like herself, wouldn't have been fooled by Miss Grim's unlikely explanation.

Bea crossed the kitchen to return the pickle jar to the refrigerator while licking the last traces of salty juice from her lips. Carrying a plate of sugar cookies, Bea padded out of the kitchen on her thickly bandaged feet and headed for Lila's rocking chair.

Bea was prickling with curiosity to know what Walter meant when he'd stood at the door and told Lila that he had important news for Bea.

The comic section from that morning's *Oregonian* newspaper was spread across the trunk. Bea set the plate of cookies on top of the newspaper, being careful not to cover up the Mickey Mouse cartoon strip.

Earlier, she'd left a pad of drawing paper and a box of crayons on the carpet next to the rocker. She set the paper on her lap. After a studied glance at the newspaper, she pushed up the lid of the crayon box and chose a red crayon. The pure enjoyment of drawing soon occupied her thoughts and her earlier restlessness faded.

Alone in the apartment, the early hours of the afternoon passed peacefully, moved along by the rhythmic ticking of the clock and the hushed 'Shhh, Shhh', sounds of crayons on paper.

Bea was holding up a stubby white crayon, and using her thumbnail to scrape away the speckled bits of other crayons that dotted its blunt end, when there was a series of sharp staccato knocks on the front door.

Recognizing Walter's distinct knock, Bea called, "Come in," while twisting around in the rocker to face the door.

Entering, Walter's rapid, loping steps quickly carried him across the room. He sat rather stiffly on the sofa.

"Hi," Bea said.

"Hi, yourself." Walter hesitated, then asked, "How are your feet?"

"They hardly hurt at all. They're more itchy than anything else."

"That's good," Walter said uneasily. He avoided looking directly into Bea's face, instead, glancing around the room and down at the floor while he talked.

Bea guessed he was feeling partly to blame for her accident and was unsure of what to say. Although there was a certain pleasure in watching him squirm, she decided to let him off the hook.

"Sure was a dumb thing I did," Bea stated flatly.

Her admission brought about an immediate and visible relief in Walter.

Walter's shoulders relaxed and his eyes finally met Bea's. A relieved grin spread across his face. His teeth gleamed in his deeply tanned face and his cap of pale blonde hair shone in stark contrast to the sofa's smooth, red silk.

With his normal good spirits restored, Walter grabbed a sugar cookie off the plate and took a bite.

"What's up?" he mumbled, while chewing.

"I'm drawing comics. Yesterday Lila explained to Bell about my feet, so Bell would understand when I didn't show up for work in the laundry. This morning Bell stopped by to give me the get-well cards her children made for me. Now I'm drawing pictures in return to thank them."

"Let me see?"

Walter reached for the stack of finished drawings, looking thoughtfully at each one.

"They're really good," he admitted. He pointed to a drawing of Minnie Mouse with long, fluttery eyelashes, wearing a red polka dot dress. Her round feet were stuffed into a pair of spiky red shoes.

"I think you're starting to turn into Minnie Mouse," Walter teased, "at least in the feet."

Bea looked down at her feet. "You're right," she agreed heartily, lifting her feet and plopping them down on top of the trunk.

When Lila had bandaged Bea's burned feet she'd wrapped each foot in layer after layer of soft cotton strips. Over the cotton she'd pulled on a pair of thick wool socks, finishing with ribbed, dark grey knit slippers.

"Thank goodness I don't need to stuff these into a pair of tiny shoes with pointy toes."

"Let me know if you start to grow a tail," Walter said. He reached for another cookie and popped it whole into his mouth.

"Walter, there's something I've been waiting to tell you. I'm sure I've discovered more evidence for our case against Miss Grim."

"I bet your evidence isn't as important as what I've discovered. But you go first."

Bea leaned forward in her chair.

"You probably heard that it was Miss Grim who found me sitting along the side of the road. When she was standing right there beside me, before she left to get help, I noticed she had a pair of wire cutters in her pocket. When she realized I'd seen them, she looked flustered and mumbled something about returning them to Jiggs. She claimed she'd seen them fall off the back of his wagon."

Walter swallowed and used his shirtsleeve to wipe sugar from his mouth before he replied.

"Why would stuck-up Ol' Grim do Jiggs a favor?"

"Exactly my point.

"I know there has to be another reason why she was walking down that dusty road to the dairy barn," Bea insisted. If there are two things Miss Grim is sure to avoid, besides children, it's animals and dirt."

"She's hiding something," Walter agreed. But, if she was stealing the wire cutters, why was she going to the barn?"

Bea shrugged, wrinkling her forehead. "That's the part I can't figure out.

"Okay, Walter, it's your turn now. So what's the big secret?"

Bea reached for a cookie, but her fingers brushed across an empty plate.

"Weelll," Walter began slowly, although the gleam in his eyes betrayed his eagerness.

"You're not the only one who saw Miss Grim acting strangely that day. While my family was eating supper, the doorbell rang. Mom got up from the table to answer the door. After a bit, I heard Mom reply, "We'd be glad to help. Wait here a moment."

"From my place at the kitchen table I have a clear view

into the living room and I saw Mom pick up something off dad's desk."

"Did you see what it was?" Bea interrupted.

"You'll find out. Let me finish," Walter flared.

"Anyway, as soon as Mom stepped back into the kitchen, I asked her who was at the door."

"Miss Grim," Bea was about to guess, although she hadn't quite gotten the words out of her mouth before Walter yelled out, "Bingo," slapping the top of the trunk for added emphasis.

Bea's feet bounced from the impact. Walter's shout, coming so unexpected, startled Bea and set off an attack of hiccups. Bea slapped her hands over her mouth. Walter laughed uproariously. But then he had to wait to continue his story, while Bea plugged her nose and held her head upside down between her knees, trying to squelch the hiccups.

When she finally lifted her head, gasping for air, her face and neck were bright red. After a moment of calming breaths, the color in her face had faded to a pale pink flush and the hiccups hadn't returned.

"Well, what did your mom give her?" Bea asked, anxious to continue.

"Guess," Walter smirked.

"Walter, I'm not going to guess."

"It was a key to Dad's car. Miss Grim's car wouldn't start and because she had an important meeting that night, she wanted to borrow our car. Miss Grim said she'd be leaving soon, but would only be gone for an hour.

"Did she say where she was going?"

"Mom didn't ask. But then during dessert, while I was pouring milk on my bread pudding, I started thinking it would be fun to be a fly in the car and spy on her. Then I thought, well why not.

125

"I gobbled down my dessert, which I usually do anyway, so it didn't look suspicious, and told my folks I would be outside for a while, messing around at the clubhouse. Instead, I ran around to the garage, climbed into the back seat of our car and lay down on the floor. I covered myself with a blanket and several coats I'd grabbed on my way out.

Bea stared at Walter. An astonished look on her face.

"Weren't you scared?"

"Only that I'd get caught and my Dad would give me a lickin'.

"I was lucky," Walter boasted. I just got settled when the front driver's side door opened and closed. The car started and backed out of the garage."

At this point in his story, Walter's voice dropped and adopted a mysterious air. Bea's hands tightened their grip on the arms of the rocking chair.

"With my ear pressed to the floor boards, I could hear the gravel crunching under the wheels as the car made it's way down the driveway. Once out on the highway we only drove a short distance before the car slowed down and turned onto a side road. The car crept ahead a short distance and stopped.

"I waited while she climbed out of the car and when I couldn't hear her footsteps any longer I threw back my cover and peeked out the window.

"Boy, was I surprised when I realized where I was."

"Where were you?" Bea almost whispered.

"In the visitor parking lot outside the front gates at the county prison."

"Prison?" Bea's jaw dropped open. "Are you sure?"

"Sure I'm sure. The buildings are completely surrounded by high wire fences. Besides, I've been there before. It's the same prison that Jiggs delivers milk to."

Bea relaxed her grip on the arms of the rocker and sat back.

"Then what happened?"

"Nothing, I covered up again and waited about half an hour before Miss Grim returned to the car and drove home."

His tale over, Walter absentmindedly reached out toward the empty cookie plate before dropping his hand in his lap.

"Miss Grim is a nurse. Maybe someone was sick and they asked her to help?" Bea suggested.

"Nah. The prison has an infirmary with their own doctors and nurses."

"We both agree that Miss Grim has done some strange things lately," Bea said. "But we still haven't found anything to prove she's a thief. We can't go to your father until we have some real evidence."

Bea shifted on the rocker in order to reach into her pocket and pull out a small, red, paper notebook. She flipped open the cover.

"Yesterday," she explained, "I was remembering that the detectives I've read about in books always keep track of their clues by writing them down on paper. So, I decided to make a list of all the evidence we'd collected so far.

Bea held up one hand and tapped each finger as she read from the list in her notebook underneath the title, The Case of Miss Grim.

"1. Suspect left two items at a pawnshop around the same time that a clock and a pipe are discovered missing.

"2. Suspect took a bundle of men's clothing into her apartment after she told two witnesses the clothes were for men in the dormitory.

"3. Suspect's parents die in a house fire.

"4. Suspect is seen in a very unlikely location with a pair of wire cutters in her pocket. Her explanation is doubtful."

Bea stopped reading while she wrote in Walter's new clue.

"5. Suspect is seen visiting a prison."

"That's a good one," Walter called over his shoulder as he left the sofa and headed for the kitchen.

"It doesn't prove anything, Walter."

"I've got one," Walter said, turning around. "How about, Suspect has the meanest face this side of the Rio Grande."

"Very funny Walter."

Bea handed Walter the notebook. He studied it a bit, then just shrugged his shoulders.

"Got me," he said, returning the notebook to Bea.

"Do you think Lila would care if I had another cookie?" Walter asked, "I'm starved."

"You're starved! Bring me one too."

Walter returned with a fistful of cookies and handed one to Bea.

"Let's go outside. We could look for Jiggs and ask him about the wire-cutters."

"I'm not supposed to leave the house. Lila wants to unwrap my feet tonight and make sure they're healing properly before she'll let me go anywhere."

"Well, we could go down to the porch. That wouldn't be leaving the house. Come on."

"I suppose that will be all right."

Bea's thickly padded feet made each step feel like she was walking on sponges. She giggled as she followed Walter down the stairs.

Bea sat on the porch steps with her chin on her knees and watched an ant dragging a cookie crumb, that Walter had dropped, along the plank step, until the ant, and it's prize, dropped out of sight over the edge. Walter swatted at a bee. The bee flew away briefly, but then spiraled back down and hovered near Walter's left ear.

"We could play Jacks," Bea suggested.

"I have a better idea," Walter said, jumping off the porch

and starting out across the front lawn. "I'll be right back," he hollered, as he ran off in the direction of the dormitory.

On the porch, where there had been a lone ant earlier, there were now many ants. Bea brushed the few remaining crumbs from her lap onto the step and watched the ants scurrying and climbing over one another in their haste to haul them away. She looked up when she heard the sounds of someone approaching.

Walter was back, pushing a wheelchair.

"Hop aboard, I'll give you a ride."

"I'd better not. Lila was serious when she said I was not to step one foot outside this house."

"That's my point. You won't be stepping on even one toe. You'll be riding."

Walter turned the chair around and backed it up to the porch.

"Jump aboard," he beckoned playfully.

"Maybe a short ride," Bea said, rising off the porch. She climbed into the chair, her legs raised and sticking out in front.

"All set," Bea said.

"And be careful Walter, not too fast. I'd have a hard time explaining to Lila how I got hurt falling out of a rocking chair in the sitting room."

After a good hard push, helped along by a Tarzan call, Walter, the chair, and Bea started across the yard, the chair picking up speed as it rolled through the gate.

Out on the driveway, the wheels spun and slipped in the loose gravel. Bea bounced on the seat and screeched. But once they reached the lush lawn surrounding the dormitory the chair rolled along with ease.

When they passed the dormitory's east porch, Bea waved heartily at the porch sitters. Even though most of them appeared to be asleep in their chairs. One lady lifted a hand-kerchief from her lap and waved it.

Walter pushed the chair around and around, circling the trunk of the largest tree. When they were both slightly dizzy, Walter pulled up and dropped to the grass to catch his breath. Bea closed her eyes while waiting for her queasy stomach to settle.

"Look over there," Walter said, climbing to his feet. "Someone's inside the morgue."

Bea opened her eyes and looked across the lawn to the small building that stood at the base of the water tower. Usually the building was closed up tight. Today the window shades were drawn up and someone was moving around inside.

Over the summer Bea had walked past the morgue many times with out giving it much notice. But now, she experienced the same uneasy chill she'd felt when Walter showed it to her that first day on the farm.

"Maybe they're cleaning it up because someone died," Walter said with unrestrained glee.

Bea gaped at Walter in astonishment.

"Oh, I didn't mean I'm glad someone died. But I've been waiting for the chance to see Picket's ghost."

"Who?" Bea questioned.

"Mr. Picket's ghost. I heard about the ghost from John, the man who scrubs pots in the kitchen. John's lived here longer than anybody and knows everything that's ever happened."

"What did happen?"

"About ten years ago, a Mr. Picket who roomed up on the third floor, died in his sleep. John and another man loaded the body onto a stretcher to carry it out to the morgue. They were starting down the last flight of stairs when the man in front slipped and let go of the front end of the stretcher. The body kept right on going and John found himself holding the back end of an empty stretcher."

Walter chuckled. "Ol' Mr. Picket sailed down those stairs lickety-split, slid across the hall and came to rest in a sitting position leaning against the drinking fountain."

Bea couldn't help laughing.

"John says that whenever anyone dies Picket's ghost returns and hovers above the body until it's safely inside the morgue."

"Has John seen the ghost?" Bea asked.

"He wouldn't say. But he swears it's a true story." Walter insisted.

"Maybe," Bea said. "I don't know if I believe in ghosts. Anyway, we need to get back before Lila catches us."

"I sure would like a chance to see that ghost," Walter said, taking hold of the wheel chair and turning back toward home.

CHAPTER
15

It had been two days since the bandages had come off and Bea was once again wearing her regular socks and shoes. Bell had heartily welcomed her back to work, purposely assigning Bea chores at the folding table for most of the morning, allowing Bea to sit and rest her feet.

Stacks of neatly folded pillowcases, washrags and dust cloths covered the surface of the table where Bea sat. Bea fanned herself with a handkerchief while she listened impatiently for the ringing of the bell signaling lunch break.

To pass the time she pictured the bell tower atop the roof of the three-story dormitory building, the tower's squat square sides jutting into the blue sky. The bellringer would be climbing the stairs until he stood next to the thick rope hanging down from inside the tower. Reaching up as high as he could, he'd grasped the rope in both hands.

'Clang! Clang! Clang!'

Bea jerked, startled by the intrusion of the actual bell ringing.

Bea tossed the handkerchief onto the table and headed for the stairs. She'd promised to meet Walter at the clubhouse at noon and she still had to stop off at the apartment to pick up the lunch she'd packed that morning.

As she made her way to the clubhouse she could see men streaming in from the fields, headed for the dining hall.

Arriving at the clubhouse just behind Walter, she saw him drop through the low door and disappear inside. Bea followed, ducking awkwardly through the low opening while holding her lunch.

Once she was settled on her blanket she set the apple aside, unfolded the cloth napkin wrapped around a cheese sandwich and began to eat.

"I already ate," Walter said.

While Bea chewed, Walter poked around inside an old bucket wedged into the vines at the back of his space. He eventually picked out one of the arrows he'd whittled earlier from a thin branch. Keeping the arrow, he crawled back and lay out on the ground with one arm bent to cushion his head.

Bea savored the sweet cloying smell of the sun-soaked berries ripening among the vines that formed the roof of the clubhouse. She was glad Walter hadn't worked at the dairy yet today, bringing with him the sharp barn odors that clung to his boots and pants.

When Bea was alone in the clubhouse she liked to close her eyes and lie perfectly still, lulled almost to sleep by the low contented humming of the honeybees at work. But the honeybees would find little contentment today, not with Walter present.

Walter thrust his arrow sword-like above his head, swatting at the vines and sending the bees scurrying about, buzzing loudly.

"Seen any ghosts lately?" Bea asked Walter, hoping to distract him.

"Nope. But I'll be ready when the time comes."

Walter sat up and tossed the arrow back into the box.

"Now that your feet are so much better, do you think Lila would let you go swimming?"

"I don't see why not. She's always telling me to keep my feet clean. But I have to work this afternoon."

"It doesn't get dark until late. Let's go ask my Dad if he'll take us to the Sandy River tonight."

"Cross your fingers," Bea joked as they emerged from the clubhouse and sprinted for Mr. Briggs' office. Worn without laces, Bea's tennis shoes slapped the ground as she chased after Walter.

There was no one sitting at the reception desk when they entered the small waiting room fronting the hall that led to Mr. Briggs' private office.

"His secretary must be at lunch," Walter said.

Briggs' office was situated at the end of a short hallway just beyond the reception desk. The door to his office was ajar.

"Shh!" Walter cautioned before they tiptoed past the desk. "We'll just peek in and see if he's busy."

Bea nodded.

As it turned out, they didn't need to see beyond the office door because the sounds of conversation were clearly audible in the hallway outside.

One voice belonged to Walter's father. The other voice was a woman's, softer and quivery. Bea hardly recognized the usually jovial voice of her friend from the laundry.

"Bell," she mouthed silently to Walter.

Feeling only slightly guilty, and a great deal curious, they stayed and listened.

"Do you have an explanation?" Mr. Briggs asked.

"Sir," Bell paused to blow her nose, "I've never done this kind of thing before. I was desperate to keep my family together. I know that's no excuse for what I did. My husband just picked up and left the kids and me a few months back. Without him earning some money, I just wasn't making enough to get by."

"Isn't there anyone, family maybe, that you might have appealed to for help?"

"My parents live up near Seattle. I just couldn't swallow my pride and go to them for help. They were opposed to my marriage in the first place. They said his type could never be depended upon. But I was so smitten with love, I just ran off with him anyway."

A moment of silence was broken by a jarring screech when Mr. Briggs leaned back in his chair. He made a 'humph' sound deep in his throat before he spoke.

"I'm sorry for all your trouble Bell. You've been a good employee. But, I caught you myself in the act of stealing. I can't condone it. And you've freely admitted to previously taking a clock and my pipe."

"Believe me Mr. Briggs, if I could get the things back, I would. But they are sold to my landlord and the money spent."

"I can't keep you as an employee here any longer. I have to fire you. Make sure my secretary has your address and we'll pay any wages you're owed up until today."

"Mr. Briggs, believe me, I'll never do anything like this again. I know you could have turned me into the police. What would have happened to my sweet children then?"

"Bell, before you leave, I hope you won't mind if I make a suggestion. Go home to your parents. You might discover they are anxious to forgive and have their daughter back."

At the sound of shuffling feet, Bea and Walter scooted back down the hall, through the waiting room and out of the building.

Their breaths were coming fast when they pulled up at

their own yard gate. Looking back the way they had come they saw Bell emerge from the building. With rapid steps she fled, wiping her cheeks with the corners of her apron.

She quickly crossed the short distance to the laundry and went inside. When she emerged, a short while later, she was no longer wearing the apron, but carried her purse in front of her, clutched tightly in both hands. She kept her head down as she crossed the clearing and set off down the path leading to the trolley stop. The tall, dry grass in the field swayed as she passed.

"Well, Rats!" Walter spit out, giving the gate a push with his foot. "Bell's not supposed to be the thief. Now she's gone and ruined the whole thing."

"Yeah," Bea mumbled vaguely, her eyes remained fixed on the back of the retreating figure.

"Cheer up," Walter said. "First hunches aren't always right, even for Dick Tracy. And I bet that Julianne person in Paris—"

"Juliette," Bea corrected him.

"Well, then Juliette wasn't always right was she?"

"Okay," Walter continued, "so Ol' Grim wasn't the thief we thought she was. Just because we're wrong about the pond tickets, doesn't mean we should give up the entire case. What about the rest of the clues on the list? They add up to something sneaky and, well, diabolical. We just have to figure out what."

Bea wasn't thinking about the list of clues, or feeling the letdown of a bungling detective as Walter thought. Rather, she was remembering her first day at work in the laundry and Bell's welcoming smile; and the cheerful tunes Bell hummed while standing at the folding table; and the get well cards Bell's children had given her.

"I'd better get back to work," Bea managed to say as she

stepped away from the gate. Only now realizing she still held her apple. She left it on top of the fence, wedged between two pickets. She no longer felt hungry.

Up on the drying floor, Bea pushed her cart. Patiently, without much conscious thought or energy, pulling the wet linens out of the canvas sacks and pinning them to the lines. As the afternoon slowly passed she heard whispers and snatches of conversations among the other workers, but no one seemed to know the reason for Bell's sudden departure.

Finally, the last cart was empty. Bea tugged at the apron strings, wrapped several times around her waist, undoing the bow before pulling off her apron. Before she left the building she hung it on the hook next to the apron Bell had worn that morning.

Walking up to the house, Bea saw a small gathering of people in the front yard. She recognized Lila, Miss Grim, and Mr. and Mrs. Briggs. Another man, a stranger dressed in a dark grey suit, was talking. He gestured with one hand, while holding a sheet of paper in the other.

Bea stopped a few feet away from the group. To her great surprise, prominently displayed on the lapel of the man in the grey suit was the silver star of a sheriff's badge. Another man, also sporting a badge, was standing beside a black car parked on the gravel drive circling the fountain. This man had one foot resting on the car's running board, his arms dangled over the top of the open door. He noticed Bea and tipped his hat.

The paper the sheriff had been holding was now being passed among the group on the lawn. Each person in turn studied it and then shook his head. Bea noticed Miss Grim stayed at the back of the group and gave the paper only a brief glance before quickly handing it back.

The sheriff folded the paper and slipped it into the inside

pocket in his jacket.

"These two might still be hiding out in the area," the sheriff explained. "Let us know if you see or hear anything."

"We sure will," replied Walter's dad.

"You all have a nice day now," the sheriff said, before tipping his hat and returning to his car.

Once the sheriff's car left the yard, Bea hurried to Lila's side.

"What happened?" she asked, filled with dread that Mr. Briggs had decided to report Bell's crimes after all.

"Two men escaped from the county prison just down the road. Cut their way through the fence. Brothers, he said."

Bea's shoulders dropped in relief. "Does he expect they'll show up around here?"

"I wouldn't think so. They're probably as far away from here as they can get."

Lila wrapped her arm over Bea's shoulder, giving her an affectionate squeeze.

"Let's go inside. I for one am ready to put my feet up."

Mrs. Briggs stayed in the yard talking. Miss Grim retreated inside the house the instant the sheriff turned to leave.

Dinner was finished, the dishes washed and put away. Bea was settled on the sitting room floor, her head resting on a sofa cushion, listening to the radio. Lila listened from her rocking chair while her hands kept busy weaving a sturdy thread over the worn spot in the heel of a white sock; the pointed end of the needle sliding across the polished surface of the wood darning egg.

When the program finished, Bea sat up and turned off the radio. She propped the cushion she'd been using as a headrest against the sofa leg and leaned back, smoothing the folds of her dress. Listening to the radio hadn't helped to ease her troubled thoughts, as she'd hoped. Her mind kept circling back to the things she'd learned about Bell while eavesdropping at Mr. Briggs' door.

Bea thought Bell was one of the nicest people she knew. It just wasn't fair for Bell's husband to have run off like that; not caring if he left his wife and children without enough money to live on.

Bea remembered back to the day she'd learned her mother had contracted tuberculosis. She'd fallen face down on her bed, sobbing "it's not fair". She'd even told Billy that it wasn't fair for her to remain at the poor farm when he left with his friend Henry. And the depression, why that wasn't fair to anybody.

Bea looked over at Lila. Her white hair, wound in finger curls, hugged the back of her head. A few wisps, loosened from their pins, fell across her plump cheeks. Her face, tilted toward her lap as she darned, wore an expression of ease. How soft, and settled and comforting she appeared just then to Bea.

If only she could talk to Lila about what she'd overheard.

Bea thought back to her last night at home in Portland, heartsick as she packed her things to come to the farm; and to the letter from her mother with its words of encouragement.

"If you trust, even when life seems unfair, I know you will discover the wonderful things God has planned for you this summer."

A new and rather pleasing thought slowly awakened in Bea. If Lila hadn't been disappointed in her love for William, then William wouldn't have married Faye. And William and Faye wouldn't have had a daughter named Elizabeth who would grow up next door to Lila, marry Edward, and have a daughter named Bea.

In attempting to solve one kind of mystery, Bea realized, she'd been led to ponder a mystery of another kind altogether.

Lila's patch was finished. She snipped the thread and put away her needle, shaking the sock until the darning egg dropped into her lap.

"I just can't believe the first week of August has nearly slipped by," Lila said, with a shake of her head. "Why, another summer is almost over."

Bea was relieved to be drawn out of her own troubling thoughts by Lila's word.

"Yep, summer is almost over," Bea repeated, scrambling to her feet and moving next to Lila.

Bea picked up the darning egg from Lila's lap, cupping it in her hands, sliding her palms over its smooth, curved surface while she talked.

"Mom will be ready to come home any day now," Bea said, "and of course Daddy and Billy too."

"It sure will be nice to see your whole family together again. I'm looking forward to meeting your brother Billy."

"He's okay," Bea said, with a twinkle in her eye.

Lila lifted her arm, turning her wrist to read her watch.

"It's after nine o'clock. I think the only thing left to do tonight is go to bed."

Bea sighed and plopped her hands onto her hips, pretending to be annoyed. "Why do grownups get so much enjoyment out of telling kids it's time for bed?"

"I guess it's to make up for all the times our parents enjoyed saying it to us. Your turn will come."

Bea gave Lila a lingering hug before she said "good night".

Up in the loft, Bea yawned as she undressed and pulled her nightgown over her head. Even with the windows open to the night air, the room held in the warmth collected from the summer day. Bea climbed into bed and covered herself with the sheet, pushing the blanket to the end of the bed.

Before closing her eyes, she reached to the nightstand and picked up a pencil and the red notebook. She flipped to the page titled The Case of Miss Grim. She read the first clue on the list.

1. Suspect left two items at a pawnshop around the same time that a clock and pipe are discovered missing.

Now she knew Miss Grim hadn't stolen the clock or the pipe, so Bea drew a thick line through the words, crossing out the sentence. But what about the other clues: The wire cutters, the bundle of men's clothing, and the visit to the prison. Walter is right. They still seem to add up to something sneaky, but what?

Bea fell asleep determined to solve The Case of Miss Grim.

CHAPTER
16

The following morning Bea awoke feeling rested and happy in a way she hadn't felt in along time. She slapped the alarm button on the wind-up clock in time to avoid its jarring 'briiiiing', then kicked her feet free from the tumbled sheets and slid out of bed.

Her steps were lively when she crossed the room to peek outside. Although the window faced east, the tall oak trees blocked her view of the rising sun.

Kneeling at the low window, she undid the latch and pushed the screen open before sticking her head outside. Later that afternoon, the temperature was sure to climb into the eighties. But this early in the morning, the air felt sharp and cool, prickling her face and causing the hair on her bare arms to stand up.

Bea ducked back inside, re-latching the screen. Her stomach began to growl, turning her attention to breakfast. She was hopeful, and almost certain, that Lila was downstairs in the kitchen, at that very moment, preparing her favorite meal, pancakes with strawberry syrup. It was just that kind of day.

Bea hurried to dress.

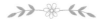

Bea's job at the laundry unfolded pretty much as usual that day. A new employee had been hired to replace Bell. A woman, who introduced herself as Gert, but had little else to say.

While Bea pushed laundry carts and pinned countless sheets to the lines on the drying floor, she thought about Bell. She hoped Bell had taken Mr. Briggs advice and returned to Seattle.

At 3:00 p.m. Bea gratefully slipped out of her work apron. Her thin cotton dress was damp with sweat and stuck to her chest and back. Inside her shoes her feet felt slick and itchy. The air in the second floor laundry was stifling hot and humid.

The Poor Farm was located on land east of Portland; an area often referred to as east county. Situated near the Columbia River, east county was routinely buffeted by the high winds that rolled out the west end of the Columbia Gorge. But on this day, though the high, screened windows on the laundry building had been propped open, not even the slightest breeze appeared to stir the air.

Instead of taking the stairs, Bea rode the service elevator down to the first floor, squeezed in between two bags of bath towels. Her early morning feelings of wellbeing had lingered throughout the day, in spite of the heat, and even now lightened her steps as she left the building and sprinted across the grounds.

At the house, Bea reached to open the door, then stepped back in surprise when the front door was jerked open from the inside. Walter emerged. He brushed past without a word, and stalked off. Bea closed her mouth, swallowing the greeting she'd intended before she saw the scowl on his face.

"Don't worry about him," offered Mrs. Briggs, who was standing in the entry. "He's just pouting because he wasn't on the spot yesterday when the sheriff stopped by with the news about the prison escape."

Well, that explains it, Bea thought, knowing all too well Walter's pressing need to be at the center of things.

Mrs. Briggs disappeared inside her apartment and Bea hurried upstairs.

The sun was setting and Bea had just turned on the lamp in the sitting room when Walter's special knock came at the apartment door. Bea moved to let him in.

"Hey, Bea. Evening Lila," Walter said, taking a few steps inside the room.

"My parents are having a card party," he announced, directing his comment to Lila. "My Dad's tired of me hanging over his shoulder. He sent me to see if Bea could come down to our apartment to keep me company."

"Could I, Lila," Bea begged. "I'm not a bit tired."

"I can't see it would hurt anything, tomorrow being Saturday. But don't the pair of you bother the grownups."

"We won't. Thanks Lila."

Downstairs, Walter stopped outside his apartment and grabbed Bea's arm. "Stay here and be quiet," he ordered.

"Why? Aren't we going inside?"

"Shhh I'll explain in a minute."

Walter entered his apartment alone. He stopped when he was only a few feet inside and yelled, "Lila said it's okay for me to stay." He quickly came back out and closed the door.

Bea looked puzzled. "I thought we were staying at your house?"

"Keep quiet," Walter whispered, "and come on."

He stepped quietly across the hall and eased the front door open. He slipped outside. Bea followed, closing the door with caution, unconsciously caught up in Walters' furtive behavior.

Walter was already hustling down the front walk, but Bea remained stubbornly on the porch, her arms crossed in front of her.

"Wait!" she demanded indignantly.

"Shhhh!" Walter frowned.

Bea continued in a loud whisper. "I'm not going anywhere until you tell me what's going on,".

Walter turned and came back to the porch steps.

"My parents think we're upstairs at your apartment. And Lila thinks we're downstairs at mine. It's perfect. No one will miss us.

"Miss us? Where are we going?"

"Do I have to explain everything to you?"

"Yes, you do."

"It's true my parents are having a card party. And it's true I was hanging around and pestering my Dad. It's a lucky thing I was there, too. One of the nurses called from the dormitory to let Dad know a man who roomed on the third floor had died in his bed."

"Oh, no. Was it someone I knew."

"No, it was a new guy, just arrived."

"Anyway, Dad sent back a message for the staff to wait until after dark, when most of the other residents are in their rooms, before taking the body around to the morgue."

"That's too bad, I mean about the man dying" Bea said. "But what does that have to do with us?"

"Don't you get it. We're going to hide and watch for Picket's ghost."

Bea dropped her arms, a look of pure astonishment on her face.

"We're….Ghost…." she stuttered.

"You're not scared are you?"

"No, I'm not scared," Bea answered, trying to put more confidence in her voice than she really felt. "It's just that I don't believe there is a ghost."

"That's why we have to do this. Now's our chance to find out for sure. Are you coming?"

Bea hesitated, glancing back over her shoulder.

"Oh, all right."

Bea followed Walter out of the yard, turning outside the fence in the direction of the dormitory. Almost unconsciously, they'd slipped into their detective roles, stepping carefully on the loose gravel, trying not to make any noise.

The farm was settled down for the night, quiet, except for the croaking of frogs; one sound that Bea had come to associate with nights in the country. At the southern end of the farm, beyond the dairy barn, there was a deep pit in the ground filled with murky, green water. Although not suitable for swimming, Jiggs said it was a little bit of heaven for frogs. One time Bea had asked Jiggs why she never heard the frogs croaking during the day. He'd said it was because the frogs were natural born braggarts and didn't like competition from the other animals.

Once Bea and Walter moved outside the reach of the porch light darkness quickly enveloped them, giving everything familiar an eerie disguise. Bea tried to ignore the disquieting sensation that she and Walter weren't the only ones hiding out, waiting for Picket's ghost.

They stepped cautiously until they came alongside the

dormitory. Lights were turned on in many of the rooms, giving the flat, three-story façade a checkered appearance. In some of the windows, shadows moved behind the thin paper shades. The double front doors at the back of the ground floor porch remained firmly shut. No one appeared outside the building. As they watched, some of the lights blinked out.

"Are we just going to wait here to see the ghost?" Bea whispered.

"We can't," Walter explained. They might carry the corpse out the back door. We'd miss it if we stayed here. I've thought of a place to hide that's perfect. Come on."

They were almost past the building when a high-pitched, creaking noise drifted out from the shadowed depths of the dormitory porch.

Startled, Bea gasped, bumping into the back of Walter who'd come to a sudden stop. Walter's eyes were widened in surprise.

For a few seconds they remained like statues, too afraid to move. Then, slowly they looked back over their shoulders, their eyes probing the depths of the shadowy porch. Bea's heart beat rapidly in her chest.

What Bea saw on the porch made her stomach clench and her knees go all loose and shaky.

The white painted rocking chairs, spread over the length of the porch, seemed to rise out of the gloom, their high slatted backs illuminated in moonlight. As Bea and Walter stared, transfixed, the chair at the far end of the line slowly tipped forward and then settled back. Just like dominos falling in turn, the next chair rocked forward and then back, and the next; each one creaking in protest.

As they stared in disbelief, a small dark shape appeared on the floorboards. It crept forward in a hopping motion to the edge of the porch, stopping on the top porch step. Briefly, two red eyes glistened and blinked. Then the dark mound leaped off the step into the bushes and disappeared.

Not realizing she'd been holding her breath, Bea suddenly let out a loud whoosh of air.

It's on…, only a rabbit," Walter stuttered.

Bea giggled nervously.

"Come on," Walter said.

Bea took a final look at the place in the bushes where the rabbit had disappeared before moving away.

CHAPTER
17

The fright Bea and Walter had experienced outside the dormitory had left Walter with a good deal less bravado than he'd managed earlier back at the house.

In a slightly more subdued manner, they approached the laundry building. During the daylight hours, when Bea was at work, the laundry was a bustling and noisy place; a chaotic blend of voices and footsteps, opening doors and closing cupboards, squeaks and groans from washing machines and laundry carts. Sounds echoed throughout the building, eventually drifting outside through the opened windows on the drying floor.

In the dark of night the building loomed unfamiliar, menacing and deserted. Bea searched for the dark square of Lila's office window.

The building seemed to be holding its breath, waiting along with her and Walter for something ominous to happen? The idea sent shivers running up Bea's back.

After turning the corner at the end of the building they came to an abrupt halt. Up ahead, directly across from the ice storage shed and loading dock stood the morgue. A small, one room building that at first glance might oddly enough be mistaken for a child's playhouse.

Inside the morgue the lights had been turned on.

"Do you think we're too late?" Bea whispered. "Maybe they've already put the body inside, and the ghost left."

"If there was a ghost," she mumbled under her breath. Although she was beginning to fear that it was entirely too possible.

"I'll go find out," Walter answered, "I'll look inside."

Bea walked with Walter as far as the storage shed, where she waited leaning against the dock. Walter hunched down and crept ahead. He came up to the morgue directly beneath a window. Sitting back on his heels, he twisted around and waved at Bea. A mischievous grin spread across his face. The light spilling out the window above his head cast his eyes and nose in shadow, giving his face a skull-like appearance.

Bea motioned for him to hurry.

Grasping the windowsill with his fingertips, Walter slowly raised himself. After a brief look, he stepped away from the building and jogged back to where Bea waited.

"The place is empty," Walter spit out.

"Now what?" Bea asked.

"We'll wait right here until someone shows up with the body. And the ghooooost," he added, in a quivery voice.

Walking up to the dock, Walter raised his hands to chest height, placing them on the platform and jumped, landing on his stomach with a 'humph'. He scrambled to his feet. Bea crawled up after him.

They moved back into a dark corner, where the dock joined up to the shed. It was the perfect spot to hide, stay out of sight, and have a clear view of the morgue and anyone who might be approaching.

During the day the dock area was in constant use.

Vegetables were lugged up from the fields in crates and stacked on the dock to be stored amongst the blocks of ice inside the shed. The floor was littered with debris.

Bea sat down on the worn planks next to Walter, but immediately lifted up to pluck, from beneath herself, a shriveled leaf and a slimy green bean. She tossed the squashed bean off the end of the dock and brushed a clear place to sit. When she was finally settled, she leaned back against the large sliding door that opened into the shed.

Walter, Bea knew, was determined to wait out the ghost no matter how long it took, but after a few minutes his determination was greatly tested by his ineptitude for sitting still. To pass the time he began a thorough and systematic scratching of all his mosquito bites.

'Scritch! Scritch! Scritch!'

Bea tried to ignore him by concentrating on the deep-toned bellowing of the bullfrogs. Bats darted about in the night sky. Their movements so swift in the darkness overhead that their presence was more often sensed than actually seen.

Bea let her head sink back against the door and closed her eyes. Her thoughts drifted back to other summer evenings. Times when she, along with her parents and her brother Billy, would gather in their backyard to escape the stifling heat inside the house. While the grownups sipped iced tea, sitting on chairs they'd carried outside from the kitchen, she and Billy would lay out on a blanket spread in the grass. Billy and Bea always competed to be the first to locate the North Star.

Bea was abruptly pulled back to the present when she heard a heavy thud coming from inside the shed. A startled gasp, more like a hiccup, escaped from her lips.

Walter stopped scratching. His curled fingers frozen in place on top of his knee. Bea's breath caught in her throat and she instinctively scooted away from the door. A door, that was the only thing separating her from whatever had moved inside the shed.

Walter swiveled around and stared unblinking at the door as if he could will himself to see through the boards to the inside.

They waited in strained silence, but the sound wasn't repeated.

Bea spoke first, comforting herself with what she hoped was a logical and safe explanation. "It could be the rabbit again, looking for food."

"Maybe. Or it could be a rat," Walter quipped.

Bea grimaced and shuddered.

"It's true," Walter insisted. "I've seen Jim set traps. They tunnel their way in."

"If it is a rat, at least it won't be looking to come out this door."

"No, but Picket's ghost might."

"Walter, you said that the ghost hovers above the dead body until it's safely carried inside the morgue. So, why would Picket's ghost be inside the shed?"

"I don't know. It's possible. Maybe it got lost or hungry."

"Not likely, Walter. Besides, ghosts don't knock into things, they pass through them."

Walter opened his mouth, hesitated and closed it. The logic of her statement defied argument, so he turned away to resume scratching.

Bea rubbed her arms and wished she'd thought to bring a sweater. The temperature had dropped noticeably. A cool gust of air swirled around the corner of the shed, scooting dried leaves across the dock.

Scritch! Scritch!

"Must you do that?" Bea moaned.

"Yep," Walter answered.

Bea wrapped her arms around her legs and rested her chin on her bent knees.

"If someone doesn't show up soon," she said, "I'm leaving. I never believed in Picket's Gh….."

Bea's complaint was cut short by a sharp poke in her side from Walter's elbow.

Beside her, Walter stiffened; his eyes wide and fixed on something out there in the darkness. Bea looked to the right, following the direction of his gaze, squinting and craning her neck for a better look.

At the very spot where Bea had stopped earlier to look up at Lila's office window, a dark grey shape began to materialize out of the blackness. A figure whose features were hidden inside what appeared to be a long, hooded cloak.

As they watched, the mysterious figure loomed larger, taking hesitant steps in their direction.

Walter leaned in close to Bea. "Is it the ghost?"

"I don't think so. Do ghosts wear cloaks?"

"How would I know? If it's a person can you see who it is?"

"Noooo. But it sure isn't a rabbit."

Bea's remark served to break the tension and set them both into a fit of nervous giggles. They quickly lowered their heads, slapping their hands over their mouths to muffle the sounds.

When Bea looked up again the figure had moved closer, but was now standing just outside the reach of light fanning out from the morgue windows. The cloak's deep hood was pulled forward, concealing the face. Whoever, or whatever it was, had their arms wrapped awkwardly around a large bulge pushing out from underneath the front of the cloak at the waist.

"Do you think it heard us?" Bea whispered.

Walter shrugged his shoulders. "It can't see us if we just sit still."

"What if it comes up on the dock?"

"Why would it come up here?"

"I don't know, we did."

Images of Lila's warm, cozy apartment, with herself curled up on the sofa, flooded Bea's mind. Why had she ever let Walter talk her into this ghost hunt?

Walter and Bea exchanged fearful glances.

Was Walter thinking about his own apartment?

A deep silence fell over the yard. It seemed to Bea that she could almost hear her heart, it beat so rapidly beneath her shirt.

The cloaked figure waited as mysterious and unmoving as a statue.

Then, without warning, a narrow beam of light sliced through the darkness at their backs. Walter and Bea turned to face the bobbing stream of light that was growing steadily brighter.

Bea looked back over her shoulder in time to see the mysterious figure slip into the shadows between the camellia bushes that grew along the foundation of the laundry.

The man's voice was low and deep and carried crystal clear in the still night air.

"Hold that flashlight steady. Can't see where I'm putting my feet. I don't want to take a tumble with this body."

"It's them," Walter yelped. "Now I'll prove there really is a ghost."

Caught up in the excitement of the moment, Walter didn't even notice he was holding Bea's hand. Suddenly the night became still. Even the frogs were silent as if they too were focused on the corner of the building where any moment the men transporting the corpse would step into view.

Would they finally see Picket's Ghost?

Neither Walter or Bea noticed when high up on the shed

wall, the metal wheels attached to the door began to roll, or heard the faint screech of metal, or noticed the door at their backs slowly begin to open.

CHAPTER
18

Kneeling on the dock, Walter and Bea were oblivious to the rough planks as they waited for the men carrying the body to appear.

The farm staff orderly's white cotton shirts and pants made them easy to spot when they finally stepped out from behind the shed. Two men carried the body on a stretcher, their arms stiff at their sides bearing the weight of the cloth-covered mound laid out between them. A flashlight protruded from the armpit of the man in front. Its beam of light bobbed and swayed to the rhythm of their steps.

Walter leaned toward Bea, placing his head close to hers. "Can you see the…"

Whatever Walter intended to say was cut short, reduced to a startled wheeze when a pair of strong hands with thick, stubby fingers grabbed hold of the back of his shirt. A quick jerk and Walter found himself being dragged backwards across the dock toward the now open shed door.

Before Bea even had a chance to react to Walter's predicament, she too was grabbed from behind.

"I won't hurt you none," a man's voice cautioned.

Bea managed a startled, "What!" before a hand with long, knobby fingers closed over her mouth. She saw only a brief glimpse of a faded grey and white striped shirt before an arm circled her waist, and lifted her right off the dock. Bea's eyes popped wide in surprise.

Held snugly against the man's chest, Bea's feet dangled above the ground while the back of her head pressed against the bony knob of his shoulder.

From inside the shed, the man holding Walter called out in a gruff whisper.

"Don't just stand there Vern. Bring the girl inside."

"Keep you're pants on Buck," Vern drawled. "I'm coming."

After tightening his grip on Bea, Vern backed into the shed. The air in the enclosed space held the strong, earthy smells of damp vegetation and wood chips. Bea shivered at the sudden drop in temperature. Yet the touch of ice-cooled air on her bare skin shocked her into action.

Balling her hands into tight fists, Bea began flailing her arms and kicking wildly. Few of her punches connected with anything more substantial than air. But, she did manage to land one sold kick to the shin of her captor.

"Ahhhhh." Vern bellowed in pain.

His grip loosened and Bea slipped from his grasp. She landed on her bottom on top of a block of ice, as neatly as if she'd been plopped onto a chair.

Vern, the victim of her well-placed kick, hopped fitfully about the crowded space on one foot, rubbing his throbbing shin and moaning.

Walter, meanwhile, had managed to fill his hands with the sawdust that lay thick on the ice shed's floor. With his own eyes squeezed shut, he flung the sawdust over his shoulders and directly into the face of the man gripping his shirt.

Immediately there followed a howl of surprise and anger.

The hold on Walter's shirt released.

Bea heard the "thump" when Walter's head hit the floor.

"Ouch," Walter yelled. Then quickly scrambled to his feet, rubbing the back of his head.

Buck swayed on his feet. Sawdust particles coated his bushy eyebrows and short spiky hair. He sputtered and spit and clawed at the sawdust in his eyes. In his frenzied state he collided with Vern who was bent over and hopping about on one foot.

The shed's damp, sawdust strewn floor proved to be a slippery stage. Hopelessly entangled, Vern and Buck slipped and slid like a three-legged stool on an oil slick. Their feet finally lost hold with the floor and shot into the air. Thrown together in an awkward embrace, they fell into a tall stack of vegetable crates. The crates teetered and swayed.

After a moment of uncertainty, the crate on the top of the stack fell. It landed on Buck, who had landed on Vern. The crate split apart, dumping its load of carrots.

"Get off me you Oaf," Vern swore, pounding on Buck's back.

Buck grumbled a reply, scattering carrots as he flailed his arms and legs in a struggle to right himself. In the midst of all the pushing and shoving, Buck smacked Vern in the nose with his elbow. Vern responded by pelting Buck with carrots he'd grabbed up off the floor.

During all this commotion, Bea and Walter were left alone and could have escaped the shed. But they remained rooted to the spot; their fears overcome by astonishment at the comical antics of their captors.

What happened next took them all by surprise.

The grounds surrounding the morgue and dock was suddenly illuminated with light. Light spilled into the shed through the open door. At the same time there were sounds of running footsteps, slamming doors, automobile engines starting.

Accustomed to the dim light cast by the moon, the four people in the shed ducked their heads, squinting and blinking as they strained to see in the sudden brightness.

Then from somewhere out in the brightness they heard a shout and a loud voice called, "Freeze where you are." The command, amplified over a megaphone, had the sound of authority.

Bea made out the form of a man standing at the end of the dock. The man lifted the megaphone to his mouth.

"This is Sheriff Tate," he said. "You kids come on out."

Suddenly mobilized with relief, Bea slipped off the block of ice and stumbled after Walter, who was all ready sprinting across the dock. As Bea jumped to the ground, two sheriff deputies climbed up. With guns drawn, they moved in on Buck and Vern.

"You two all right?" the sheriff asked, laying a calming hand on Bea's shoulder.

"I almost had them for you," Walter informed the sheriff.

"You were a great help," the sheriff responded, grinning.

Bea merely nodded mildly. The icy-cold, wet condition of the seat of her pants was suddenly catching her attention.

Several police vehicles pulled up. Their headlights continuing to light up the scene.

Buck and Vern were escorted from the shed in handcuffs. Both men wore the grey and white, striped uniform of prison inmates. A number was stenciled on the front pocket of each man's shirt.

Standing safely in the shadow of sheriff Tate, Bea took a close look at the prisoners. Their twin-like appearance was due solely to the clothes they wore. Buck was considerably shorter and more muscular. His round face was splotchy red and scratched. He blinked continually to soothe his red, watery eyes.

Vern, Bea thought, seemed only tired and a little bit sad. His thin face looked pale beneath a rapidly swelling nose, already turning purple.

Sawdust dropped from their clothes as they walked, drifting in faint trails across the dock.

Sheriff Tate pointed to the paddy wagon, the vehicle used to transport prisoners, which had just pulled up. As the men were led away, Bea noticed a carrot's feathery green top sticking out from the cuff of Buck's pant leg.

When Bea turned to tell Walter, he'd disappeared. She looked around until she saw him next to the paddy wagon. He was jumping up and down, trying to see inside through the barred windows.

While Bea watched Walter, the prisoners were loaded and the door at the back of the wagon slammed shut with a heavy metallic ring. A deputy, using one of the keys dangling from a loop at his belt, locked the door. He motioned for Walter to move away.

"Wait over by the dock steps," Sheriff Tate said to Bea before turning away to talk to one of his deputy's. Walter reluctantly did as he was told and found Bea at the steps. A cocky grin spread across his face and Bea could tell he was feeling quite pleased with himself; As if he'd successfully arranged the whole affair.

Bea rubbed the seat of her pants, trying to ignore the discomfort.

Across the yard, she spotted Sheriff Tate striding slowly and cautiously alongside the laundry building. When he stopped, he appeared to speak into a thicket of camellia bushes. A moment later leaves rustled, and the branches parted. The mysterious figure in the long hooded coat stepped out.

Walter and Bea exchanged darting looks of recognition.

"It's, Bea stuttered.

"It's the…" Walter said at the same time.

They watched, anxious to discover the identity of cloaked figure.

The sheriff kept a firm grip on the arm of this newest and unexpected prisoner while making his way across the yard to the paddy wagon. Arriving there, the sheriff reached up and flipped back the hood on the prisoner's coat, revealing the face.

Bea's mouth dropped.

"Miss Grim?" Walter exclaimed in disbelief.

Astonished, Bea repeated, "Miss Grim?"

"I always knew she was up to no good," Walter boasted.

The sheriff was talking and as they looked on Miss Grim opened her coat and a large bundle of clothes and shoes fell to the ground. A deputy scooped them up. He stuffed them into a sack, which he tossed into the front seat of the paddy wagon before climbing in himself.

Walter was anxious to move closer.

"I want to hear what the sheriff is saying. Are you coming?"

Bea grabbed his arm.

"Walter, wait. If you call attention to yourself the sheriff just might send us back to the house."

Bea could see Walter was poised to argue, but then his shoulders dropped and he grudgingly sat down on the step.

Bea knew what she'd said to Walter wasn't entirely honest. The sheriff might have sent them away, but that wasn't the real reason she wanted to stay back.

In detective stories it had all seemed so simple. There were bad guys and there were good guys. The good guys weren't perfect, but perfect enough to be in the right. And the bad guys were always bad to the core. So when the good guys caught the bad guys and sent them to jail the good guys were perfectly glad, or nearly so. They'd won.

After a quick glance at Miss Grim, Bea stared blankly at her feet. She didn't feel like she'd won.

"Look," Walter said, drawing Bea's attention.

Miss Grim clutched her coat tightly around her before she was helped into the back of the paddy wagon. Sheriff Tate secured the lock and hit the side of the wagon with his flat hand.

The engine sputtered and caught, the headlamps came on, and slowly the paddy wagon pulled away.

As it rolled past the dock the top of Vern's head was visible through the bars in the window. Walter and Bea watched until the back of the paddy wagon rounded the corner of the laundry and disappeared from sight.

In the wake of the departing wagon, approaching from the direction of the house, hurried Mr. and Mrs. Briggs, Lila, and a man and woman Bea supposed to be the card-playing guests. Walter and Bea leaped off the steps and ran to meet them.

Lila's housedress was haphazardly buttoned, evidence of her haste in getting dressed. Having been interrupted in the midst of her preparations for bed, Lila wore a hairnet wrapped around her pin-curled hair and knotted on the top of her head. Bea thankfully slipped into Lila's warm embrace.

Mr. Briggs merely ruffled Walter's hair in passing as he strode purposely over to question Sheriff Tate.

"Walter, you've frightened me nearly to death," Mrs. Briggs exclaimed, after expelling a relieved sigh.

She drew Walter tightly to her side, burying his face into her fuzzy brown sweater. When Walter finally wriggled free, bits of brown fuzz were stuck to his lips. He wiped his mouth on his shirtsleeve.

"Mom I'm fine," he protested.

"I see you're fine, young man. And I'm certainly curious to hear your explanation for this little escapade. But right now I just want to get you home."

"I agree," Lila said. Then turning to Bea, "You feel as cold as a block of ice young lady." Lila rubbed Bea's bare arms as they walked back to the house.

While Lila hurried the children inside, Mrs. Briggs waited on the front porch to bid her guests goodnight, promising to call with a full explanation in the morning.

CHAPTER
19

Wrapped in a nightgown and robe, Bea sat curled and content in the corner of the sofa in the Briggs' living room. Bea cradled a china cup between her hands, now and then taking small sips of cocoa, drawing out the pleasure.

Across from her, Walter was perched Indian style on the seat of a stuffed leather chair enveloped in his father's flannel robe, which was quite large and draped over the edge of the chair onto the floor.

A chocolate smudge topped Walter's upper lip. He tipped his head back and tapped the bottom of his cup, catching the last remaining drops on his tongue.

As Mrs. Briggs and Lila entered the room from the kitchen, the mantel clock chimed the evening hour of ten o'clock. Mrs. Briggs held out a delicate white pitcher embellished with gold raised figures and filled with cocoa. The same pitcher that had been used to serve cocoa by Mrs. Briggs' mother and her mother's mother before that.

"Anyone ready for more?"

Walter thrust out his arm, shaking his empty cup.

His mother's raised eyebrows prompted him to add a

modest "Yes, please," followed along by a hearty, "thank you."

After Lila carefully settled down next to Bea, she blew gently into her own steaming cup of cocoa. Chocolate bubbles edged the inside lip of the cup.

Mrs. Briggs was setting the pitcher on the coffee table when they all heard the faint click of the front door opening and closing.

"Oh, Boy, Dad's home," Walter moved to slide from his chair, but his father entered the room and motioned for him to stay put.

"I'll sit over here," he said, motioning to a vacant chair.

Mrs. Briggs sat on the arm of Walter's chair.

Everyone stared at Mr. Briggs.

"Dad, were those men the bank robbers? How'd they get in the ice shed? What was Miss Grim doing? Did you...?"

Walter's mom patted his leg, interrupting his stream of questions.

"Walter, slow down, allow your father a chance to explain. I'm sure we're all anxious to hear." She looked to her husband, "Go ahead, Dear."

"You are right, Walter. The two men hiding in our shed are the same pair that escaped from prison earlier this week. They're brothers, Vern and Buck Grimesby. But there is one interesting fact the sheriff didn't tell us on his previous visit. Miss Grim is their sister.

"Sister!" the four listeners gasped.

"How sad," Lila sighed.

"No wonder she was always so secretive," Mrs. Briggs shook her head. "She must have shortened her last name from Grimesby to Grim so no one would catch on."

Bea stared into her cup, her thoughts turned back to the visit she'd made with Walter to the library. That 1900 newspaper account of a deadly house fire; Miss Grim along with two younger brothers, escaped the burning home through a window; the parents who died.

Bea left her cocoa unfinished, setting the cup on the end table. The warm liquid now sat uneasily in her stomach.

"Keep going with your story Dad," Walter urged. What else did the sheriff say?"

"Well, it seems Miss Grim helped her brothers to escape. Somehow she was able to sneak a pair of wire cutters into the prison. The brothers used them to cut holes in the security fence."

"Wire cutters?" Walter mouthed the words silently while sharing with Bea the quick, knowing glance of conspirators.

"Sheriff Tate was aware of the family tie between Miss Grim and the escaped men," Mr. Briggs continued. "He figured she was involved somehow when he showed up here with the wanted poster and she pretended not to recognize the two men. There have been deputies staked out watching the farm ever since."

"Why, those two men have probably been hiding out in the ice shed all along," Lila said.

"Most likely waiting for their sister to bring them some money and clothes," Mr. Briggs agreed.

"Yeah, clothes from the basement in the laundry building I bet," Walter quipped.

"And how would you know that young man?" Mrs. Briggs asked.

"Oops," Walter slapped his hands over his mouth and slumped down in his chair. At the same time he shot Bea a wide-eyed guilty look. "Let's tell them Bea," Walter mumbled through spread fingers. He was now so eager to spill the beans about their secret sleuthing he was unconsciously bouncing in his chair.

"All right," Bea agreed, with a touch of relief. "But I get to start."

Bea was suddenly as anxious as Walter to tell the adults.

"For a long time," Bea began, "well, at least since last winter when I started reading the story, Juliette in Paris, in the newspaper, I've dreamed of being a girl detective."

"And I read Dick Tracy," Walter interjected.

Bea narrowed her eyes at Walter before continuing.

"So when I came here and discovered I'd be sleeping in a loft just like Juliette, it seemed like I was getting my wish.

"What loft?" Lila asked. "You mean the attic?"

Bea kept on. "You can imagine my surprise when I looked out the loft window and discovered a water fountain just like the one in the plaza in Paris. And of course when Walter and I heard his mom telling Lila that someone had stolen the hall clock…"

"Walter, were you eavesdropping again?" Mrs. Briggs looked annoyed.

"I'm not sure I'm understanding any of this," Mr. Briggs bellowed, silencing everyone.

"Bea, will you please begin again? Yes, Walter, you will get a chance to explain. And this time, no interruptions."

For the next few minutes, Bea and Walter in turn, revealed the full extent of their sleuthing activities.

Bea took a short break in her story telling to duck upstairs to the loft and retrieve the list of clues they'd compiled while observing Miss Grim's odd behaviors. She passed the list around the room. Everyone agreed it was quite a remarkable fete of observation. Although Mrs. Briggs pointed out that there would be time later for a thorough discussion of the difference between sleuthing and snooping.

Walter insisted that not even Dick Tracy could have done a better job.

"Even if we didn't have it all figured out, we were on the right trail as they say," Bea laughed.

"There is one point I'm still not clear about," Mr. Briggs said. "Why were the two of you outside this evening and what were you doing at the dock?"

"Doing?" Walter's eyebrows lifted.

In the midst of all the excitement, the question of Picket's ghost had totally slipped his mind, until now.

Now slapping his forehead with the palm of his hand he dropped back in his chair in a disheartened heap.

"What in the world…?" Mr. Briggs exclaimed. He looked from Walter to his wife, who lifted and dropped her shoulders.

Now, Walter was muttering to himself. "I can't believe I missed it."

"Bea, maybe you would care to explain," Lila prompted.

Bea uncurled her legs, shifting to the front of the sofa cushion and dropping her feet to the floor. After a deep preliminary sigh she began.

"Earlier this evening, Walter overheard his dad on the phone telling someone on the dormitory staff to bring the body of the man who had died down to the morgue this evening after dark. Walter decided that would be a perfect opportunity for us to hide near the morgue and watch for Picket's ghost to appear.

"I said there wasn't a ghost, and he said this was his chance to prove the story was true. So we hid out on the dock."

Mrs. Briggs frowned and shook her head.

Mr. Briggs laughed. "Picket's ghost aye. When I was a boy, it was the ghost that hung out in old man Harney's hen house."

Walter sat up out of his slump.

"Did you see the ghost Dad?"

"Now that I won't tell you. Every boy, and girl," he nodded

at Bea, "should discover that for themselves."

"I don't know why you encourage such nonsense," Mrs. Briggs scolded.

Still grinning, Mr. Briggs rose from his chair and crossed the room to his desk to retrieve the new pipe Mrs. Briggs had purchased to replace the stolen one.

"I'm sorry I lied, Lila, about staying here in Walter's apartment," Bea said, "I didn't mean to worry you."

"I know that you didn't. And now my dear, I think it's time we took ourselves off to bed." Lila puffed out a ladylike grunt as she drew herself up from the sofa.

"I agree," said Mrs. Briggs. "Come on now, Walter." With a firm grip on his shoulders, she began steering him out of the room.

Left alone, Mr. Briggs chuckled lightly as he dipped his pipe into his tobacco pouch.

Upstairs in the loft, Bea slipped out of her robe and into bed. Lila cautiously made her way up the staircase and sat on the edge of Bea's bed.

"Well, this has been quite a day," Lila said, looking softly down at Bea and tucking the quilt around her shoulders.

"Quite a day is right," Bea said, wiggling her arms out from beneath the quilt and sitting up.

"I admit I was pretty scared when that man grabbed me and pulled me into the shed. But I screamed and kicked so hard he dropped me lickety-split."

Lila squeezed Bea's hand. "A very smart and brave thing to do."

"Yep," Bea said, "this has been the most exciting day of my whole life."

"I've lived a site more years than you and I can't say I've had many that would beat it," Lila said.

For a moment Bea drew quiet. A solemn, studied look came over her face.

"Lila, a part of me feels different than I thought I would about Miss Grim and her brothers getting arrested? I thought I would feel glad. In books that's how the detective feels when a case is solved."

"And you don't?"

"I'm not sure. It doesn't seem that simple."

"As you grow up you'll learn that few things are all one way or another."

For a moment they sat in companionable silence.

Then Bea's face brightened. She sat up tall and squared her shoulders. "I did prove to be a pretty good girl detective," she said.

"That you did," Lila agreed.

The effects of a long day were beginning to tell on Bea and her proud smile dissolved into a yawn.

Lila cleared her throat and said, "With all that's happened already today, I wonder if you are in any shape for more excitement. But, I have some news I know you've been waiting to hear.

"I received a phone call this evening from your father. He and your mother and Billy will be here tomorrow afternoon."

"Tomorrow," Bea screeched.

"Oh Lila, really, truly?"

"Yes, really, truly."

"They're coming, they're coming," Bea chanted. Energized with happiness she scrambled to her knees and bounced on the mattress.

Lila's face beamed, watching.

Bea stopped bouncing to ask, "What time will they be

here?" Without waiting for an answer, she blurted out, "I need to get up and pack."

"Hold on now," Lila placed her hands on Bea's shoulders, settling her back down on the mattress, "There will be plenty of time to pack in the morning. The thing for you to do now is to get some sleep."

Lila patted the pillow and Bea reluctantly lay back beneath the blanket, pulling it up to her chin.

"I'll never fall asleep just wishing for tomorrow to come. Just think on it Lila. Mother's well and we're going to be a family again.

"I can hardly wait for you to meet Billy. Then I want to introduce my family to Walter and Mr. and Mrs. Briggs and Jiggs. And then I'll take them on a tour of the whole farm. I'll show them the dormitory and the laundry and the barn and the cows and the pigs and Jiggs' horse, Eleanor, and…"

"Hold on there," Lila chuckled, "You're making me tired just thinking about it. Tomorrow will take care of itself."

"I want everything to be just like it was before the depression," Bea said, "before everyone worried about money and before mother got sick. And father can reopen the grocery store."

"Your father didn't mention the store on the telephone. But, I do know this. Whatever life looks like for the Beatrice Lamb family beginning tomorrow, I'm sure there will be ample opportunities for a certain girl detective.

"Pleasant dreams," Lila whispered as she got up from the bed. At the top of the stairs she tugged the string, turning out the light.

In the darkened room Bea listened to the soft plop of Lila's footsteps descending the staircase, quickly followed by the closing of Lila's bedroom door.

As it turned out, Bea's final thoughts before falling asleep were not about the following day and the much-anticipated reunion with her family. That knowledge, so longed for and new, she held deep, tucked around her heart.

Rather it was the earlier image of herself in the ice shed, escaped from her captors grasp and plopped down on a block of ice at the exact moment Sheriff Tate's voice bellowed through the megaphone, "Freeze where you are".

Bea fell asleep with a smile on her lips.

Eager to watch for her family's arrival, Bea had skipped breakfast and for most of the morning taken up a post atop the gate at the edge of the yard.

"A watched kettle never boils," Lila said, stepping out of the house onto the porch and sitting in her favorite chair.

Bea turned at the sound of Lila's voice. Then jumped down and skipped under the trellis and back across the yard to the porch steps. The pale green halo she'd woven from hop vine slipped down her forehead and settled across her nose. She carefully set it back on her head.

"I sure wish they'd hurry."

Getting only a nod from Lila, Bea returned to the gate and climbed up. She caught sight of Walter and Jigs walking across the clearing in the direction of the diary barn. Walter was talking a wild streak.

Bea waved. Jiggs looked over and hollered, "They here yet?"

"No," she hollered back. "Soon."

Lifting her arm to shade her face she peered intently down the length of the gravel drive to the highway.

Bea waited.

Whenever a vehicle approached on the highway she held

her breath, and then let it out in a disappointed whoosh when the vehicle passed by.

Finally, a dark car slowed and turned into the drive. Bea jumped off the gate. She didn't recognize the car. She moved several steps out from the fence and stood bouncing on her toes, squinting to make out the people inside. The sun filtering through the trees cast dappled shadows on the car's windshield, distorting the view inside.

Three people. Yes, definitely three people.

Was it them?

Bea's heart was pounding.

Suddenly, a passenger next to the door stuck his head outside the open car window, then his shoulders, and finally his arms, stretched out and waving.

"Billy!" Bea screeched

"They're here! They're here!" she yelled for everyone to hear, as she ran down the drive toward her family.

ABOUT THE AUTHOR

B. D. Johnson is married and living with her husband in Gresham, Oregon. They enjoy spending time with their three children and seven grandchildren.

Made in United States
Troutdale, OR
06/17/2024

20639274R00116

Made in United States
Troutdale, OR
06/17/2024

20639274R00116